CW01193095

TOKYO UNDERGROUND 2

TOY AND DESIGN CULTURE IN TOKYO

WRITTEN BY BRIAN FLYNN
PHOTOGRAPHY BY JEFF DEY
PUBLISHED BY SUPER7 MEDIA, INC.
DISTRIBUTED BY GINGKO PRESS INC..

TOKYO UNDERGROUND 2

BRIAN FLYNN / JOSHUA BERNARD / JEFF DEY

TOKYO UNDERGROUND2:
TOY AND DESIGN CULTURE IN TOKYO

Published in 2010 by Last Gasp and Super7 Media, Inc.
All text and artwork copyright ©2010 Super7 Media, Inc.
Second Edition
First Printing, April 2010

Last Gasp
777 Florida Street
San Francisco, CA 94110
Telephone: 415.824.6636
Facsimile: 415.824.1836

wholesale@lastgasp.com
www.lastgasp.com

ISBN: 978-0-86719-739-6

Written by Brian Flynn
Edited by Annie Tucker
Compiled by Brian Flynn of Super7 and Joshua Bernard of CollectionDX.com
Design by Hybrid Design, San Francisco, CA – www.hybrid-design.com
Primary photography by Jeff Dey – www.jeffdey.com
Additional photography supplied by Brian Flynn, Joshua Bernard,
  Isaac Ramos, Dave Keymont, and Mark Helm.

Super7 Media, Inc.
1427 Haight Street
San Francisco, CA 94117
USA

Telephone: 415.409.4700
Facsimile: 415.409.4703

info@super7store.com
www.super7store.com
www.super7magazine.com

info@CollectionDX.com
www.CollectionDX.com

Printed in China

CONTENTS

PREPARATIONS
- 08 INTRODUCTION
- 13 PACKING
- 16 TRAVELING
- 19 AT THE AIRPORT
- 20 CURRENCY
- 22 TRANSPORTATION
- 25 HELPFUL HINTS
- 30 PHRASES

NEIGHBORHOODS
- 34 TRAIN MAP
- 38 SHIBUYA
- 48 HARAJUKU/AOYAMA
- 62 SHINJUKU
- 66 NAKANO
- 74 KOENJI
- 84 KICHIJOJI
- 89 AKIHABARA
- 94 KOIWA/KAMEIDO
- 98 EBISU/DAIKANYAMA
- 104 SHIMOKITAZAWA

OTHER NEIGHBORHOODS
- 114 MACHIYA
- 116 AOTO
- 118 EKODA
- 120 TOYS-R-US

- 122 **TOY FESTIVALS**

FOREWORD

If there were ever a niche travel book, this is it. I am sure anyone with any "common sense" would never consider a project like this. Then again, Super7 has never really done much that makes any sense, and everything seems to work out for the better because of it. We are a bunch of stylish, misfit nerds who obsess about vintage toys, movies, punk records, hip-hop, sneakers, and half a dozen other forms of minutia that no one else in your family can relate to. If you can claim even the slightest predilection in your daily life for *Star Wars, Transformers, Godzilla, Ultraman, Macross,* or *Shogun Warriors*, or understand the terms *standard size, missile-firing, removable mask, mint on card, mint in box, DX,* or *completely trashed*, you're free to join the club.

To make this book, what were initially two separate sets of maps—one designed by *Super7* magazine, the other created by CollectionDX.com—were combined, elaborated on, and hopefully contextualized in a readable, enjoyable way. Shops old and new, as well as local landmarks, restaurants, and interesting places, were labeled and catalogued as simply as possible. In past years, these maps would have been guarded like gold, hidden away from all but the toy-geek elite. So consider this your lucky day, and go forth on an unprecedented international shopping spree.

Finally, this book represents a collaborative effort, an accumulation of ideas and resources that would not have been possible without the help of Super7's entire staff; CollectionDX's Joshua Bernard and Dave Keymont; expatriates Matt Alt, Dennis Hamann, Yuriko Shirahata, and Koji Harmon; frequent fliers Mike Johnson, Pushead, Roger Harkavay, Omar Valles, and Denise Wong; and local legend Take-Shit of Cocobat—who all walked the streets of Tokyo in confused disarray, locating all of these shops and hot spots across the city. This revised edition can be traced back to source information from all the above-mentioned folks, so say thank you next time you see any of them. We hope you enjoy reading this book as much as we have enjoyed putting it together.

So what are you waiting for? Get going!

—BRIAN FLYNN, MARCH 2010

TOKYO UNDERGROUND 2

You've decided to go to Tokyo, or at least you've thought about going. Maybe you are hoping to go. Maybe you are secretly hoping plane tickets are hidden inside this book. Maybe you picked this book up thinking it was a cookbook. Regardless of your reasons, you're here reading this now, so we owe it to each other to make this a worthwhile experience.

This book is not intended to be a be-all, end-all travel guide. If you need to know about all of the city's high points and tourist attractions, a "professional" travel book is a better bet for you. Our point is to get you to Tokyo, and then to keep you from getting lost in the city or under a mountain of travel tips. We'll show you how to get around like a seasoned local, see some sights fellow travelers will never witness (or even care about), and get you home hauling a suitcase stuffed to the gills with new loot, all with as little stress as possible.

From beginning to end, this book is structured around the process of preparing for and experiencing a Tokyo trip — we'll help you get ready, pack, fly, arrive, find your way around, and, of course, know where to go when you're there.

THE FIRST QUESTION

Why are you going to Tokyo? We're not being sarcastic; this is really important. If you don't know the reasons behind your trip, you probably won't know what to do when you get there. Sure, heading over for the adventure of it all is a blast, but at the very least, have a backup plan. Otherwise, you will spend your entire trip wandering from KFC to KFC, looking for Colonel Sanders pictures with Japanese captions. Trust us, we've done it. Do you want to go to the temples? Do you want to see the cherry blossom festival? Are you looking for the latest sneakers? Do you want premium denim? Are you looking for good sushi? Or are you looking to buy toys? Great! Now we can offer some help. But figure out how deep you want to go, because we can get real nerdy, real fast, and you'll probably only want to hang out with us for a little while, not for your whole trip.

Make a list. Check it twice. Give yourself plenty of time to hit the must-sees, and leave the rest to chance and spontaneity. On the one hand, you don't want to be so regimented that you act like a drill sergeant, but on the other hand, if you don't have enough to do, we guarantee that you will find a way to be bored, even in a city of ten gazillion people.

MYTHS

Everyone seems to have heard a myth about Japan. Yes, there are vending machines everywhere. Yes, you can buy beer from them. No, you cannot buy used women's underwear from them (at least not from the versions we've seen). Yes, the people are very nice. No, the Yakuza will not kill you if you look at them, nor will you know them when you see them. But yes, they are very real. Yes, almost everything has fish in it. Yes, they have everything you've ever wanted. No, there are not cyborgs everywhere (not yet, at least). Yes, they put fried eggs on hamburgers and eat pancakes as a dessert. And no, you don't have to eat them the same way.

COIN PURSE:
YOU CAN PICK THE MALE OR FEMALE VERSION, BUT IF YOU HAVE ONE OF THESE, PACK IT. THERE ARE A LOT OF COINS IN JAPANESE CURRENCY, AND YOU'LL BE HANDLING THIRTY-POUND POCKETFULS IN NO TIME.

HANDS FREE:
TAKE A BACKPACK FOR YOUR DAILY SHOPPING ADVENTURES. TRUST US, YOU ARE GOING TO NEED IT.

AVG SUMMER
78°F ✶ 26°C

SPRING

FALL

AVG WINTER
42°F ✶ 6°C

12 TOKYO UNDERGROUND 2

WHEN ARE YOU HEADING OVER?

We recommend fall over all other seasons. Spring is fine, but you do have to worry about rain and the coming monsoon season. Also, avoid Golden Week in early May, as most of Tokyo will close for the entire week. Winter is cold, but nothing like the North Pole, so it can make for a nice time as well, provided you take the appropriate layers. Avoid summer if you can. It's hot. Real hot. Then it's humid. Real humid. Imagine wearing thermal underwear while running a marathon in George Hamilton's tanning booth without the pearly-white teeth and the free drinks. Those darn monsoons make it rough, and you will spend a lot of time walking from place to place or on outside train lines. Hot + humid + crowded train = a Degree moment waiting to happen. That said, we wouldn't pass up a free summer trip if you want to give us one.

MONEY AND CURRENCY

To quote the Wu-Tang Clan, "Cash rules everything around me," but less than it used to. In all major areas and shops, your credit cards and debit cards should work just fine. We do recommend calling your bank ahead of time to tell them to keep your cards activated when all your purchases in Japan begin to show up on their radar. But at some point, you will invariably get a call from your bank; when it happens, don't let it dampen your spirits. Just get in touch with them and clear things up.

If you'll be dealing with vintage shops, many still prefer to deal in cash, and a few even deal exclusively in cash, so make sure to carry some if you go to any of these stores. Later in the book, we will discuss the finer points of exchange rates, coins, and bills, as well as how to use an ATM.

DOUBLE UP:
BY PACKING YOUR FULL SUITCASE INSIDE A LARGER, EMPTY SUITCASE, YOU ARE GUARANTEED TO HAVE ROOM TO BRING BACK ALL YOUR NEW PURCHASES.

A PLACE TO STAY:
YOU NEED TO WORK THIS OUT IN ADVANCE. DON'T THINK YOU CAN LOOK FOR A PLACE ONCE YOU GET THERE. IF YOU DON'T HAVE YOUR ACCOMMODATIONS INFORMATION, CUSTOMS WILL NOT LET YOU IN. NAME, ADDRESS, AND PHONE NUMBER — DON'T LEAVE HOME WITHOUT THEM.

PACKING

Let's get you packed. There are some things you should take and some things you should not. Unless you are traveling with a porter service, we recommend a backpack for your daily trips, and a rolling suitcase for traveling from the airport to the hotel. If you plan on buying lots of toys while in Tokyo, we recommend that you pack your belongings in a slightly smaller suitcase that can fit into a larger suitcase, so that you have one to stuff full of, well . . . *stuff*.

During your trip you will probably walk more than you are expecting to, and it's a good idea to take at least two pairs of shoes. That way, you can switch off shoes every day, or even during the day. You will be amazed by how much better your feet feel after changing into another pair of shoes that put pressure on different parts of your feet. By the same token, you don't need to take four or more pairs — unless, of course, your fitted hat matches only one specific pair at a time, in which case we expect you to go looking fresh to death.

CHARGERS/ADAPTERS
We have mixed emotions about these. Yes, you need them, but they never seem to work well. Go ahead and pack them; it's worth a shot. Some of the hotels that cater to Western travelers even have U.S.-style plugs that make it a non-issue, but those are very specific.

If you plan on getting any work done, take your laptop. Internet cafés have alternate keyboards that have an option to type in English, but most of the time they get stuck in all-caps mode. It is frustrating beyond belief.

FOOD
If you have special dietary needs, you need to take some of your own food just in case. Supermarkets are not readily available, and while there are plenty of convenience stores, they don't offer a lot of specialized options. For the vegetarians in our group, we make a habit of packing plenty of extra granola bars. You won't be able to take fruit into Japan, much less meat and poultry, so pack accordingly. Most everyone will be able to eat just fine, but if you are "that person," take some edible entrées for the road.

MEDICINE
If you like a specific medicine, take it with you unless it is a controlled substance. How, where, and what you can buy changes dramatically from country to country, so your brand of cold or sinus medicine and headache or pain reliever may not be available. You don't need to take a pharmacy, but a few key items may keep you going versus cooped up in the hotel, feeling miserable. One thing you *can* stock up on in Tokyo is pink grapefruit HALLS. You can't get them in the States, and they seemingly cure colds instantly.

BIG IN JAPAN
We hear it all the time: "If you have [insert item name here], the Japanese are crazy for it and will pay you tons of money for it. [Distant relative's or unknown friend's name] did it, and it paid for their entire trip." Trust us, if the Japanese want it, they already have it. In fact, they were stateside two years ago, buying the best versions of it before you even knew it was happening. This rule applies to all forms of sneakers, denim, Hawaiian shirts, toys, vintage t-shirts, records, and just about anything else you can think of. Don't believe the hype, and leave all this stuff at home.

SNACKS:
ALWAYS PACK A SNACK. YOU NEVER KNOW WHEN THE HUNGRIES WILL HIT, AND YOU MAY BE ON A TRAIN OR OFF THE BEATEN PATH WHERE A RESTAURANT IS NOT IMMEDIATELY ACCESSIBLE.

STEPPING OUT:
YOU WILL BE SURPRISED AT HOW MUCH WALKING YOU DO IN TOKYO, SO BE SURE TO PACK A CHANGE OF SHOES. YOUR FEET WILL THANK YOU.

THE PLANE RIDE
Don't let anyone lie to you: This is a long ride, but you can survive it. Most travelers start in or connect through a West Coast airport on their way over. A few other cities offer direct flights. All approximate flight times are listed to the right. The return flight is shorter than the outbound flight, which will be nice when you are ready to come home.

In most cases, your flight will be 8.10–14.25 hours long, so take a few things to keep yourself from going crazy. Books, iPods, and portable game systems are all good. Magazines tend to last a short time and take up lots of space and weight. Laptops generally have low battery life and allow you minimal room in coach. Those of you flying business class or first class may have fancy gadgets that work like magic and make time disappear, but we don't know about them.

We also recommend snacks. Plane food has never been known to be epic, so unless you normally eat very little in ten-plus hours at home, pack what you like. One or two pieces of fruit make a huge difference and help balance out the soda and chips you'll end up eating out of desperation. PowerBars and nuts are also good traveling items that take up little space.

Beyond that, plan for your flight ahead of time, and you won't get stuck watching *Lassie* on the overhead projector three times in a row. Sleeping can be tricky, too, so don't count on it unless you are related to Rumpelstiltskin or Ambien. If you are taller or larger than your typical traveler, check your airline options, as some have more legroom than others. An additional two inches can make a huge difference on a long flight.

PASSPORT:
YES, YOU NEED THIS. IT TAKES TIME TO GET ONE IF YOU DON'T ALREADY HAVE ONE. GET ON IT ALREADY, OR YOU'LL MISS YOUR FLIGHT.

DIRECT FLIGHTS	TO TOKYO	FROM TOKYO
HONOLULU	8:10	7:20
SEATTLE	10:20	8:43
PORTLAND	10:20	8:55
VANCOUVER, B.C.	10:30	9:00
SAN FRANCISCO	10:47	9:15
LOS ANGELES	11:21	9:45
DALLAS	12:55	11:35
CHICAGO	12:59	11:35
DETROIT	13:00	11:40
HOUSTON	13:30	12:00
ATLANTA	14:25	12:25
TORONTO	12:30	12:25
NEW YORK CITY	13:50	12:30
WASHINGTON, D.C.	14:05	12:30

DRY LAND
Once you land at Narita International Airport (Tokyo Airport is domestic only), your next stop (after a long walk) will be customs. Use the restroom beforehand if you have even an inkling, because the lines can be long. Hopefully you have filled out the entrance form they gave you on the plane, or pick one up here. Make sure you have your passport and know where you are staying in Japan. If you have these two things, you will most likely get in, unless you are wanted for a crime (that they know of). There is no visa fee, so smile, say hello, get stamped, and head off to get your luggage. Once you collect your belongings, you will go through another set of customs. Make sure you throw out your fruit here (they have a place to toss it and anything else you need to). Everyone is nice, so just act cool, and everything will be fine. Wheel on out to the exit and begin your adventure.

MONEY
Once you exit customs, you are in the Narita International Airport, and officially in Japan. Conveniently located on either side of you should be currency exchange desks, which we usually use, as the rates are good. You will need to fill out a form for types of currency and then get in line, the first of many. When it is your turn, place your money and form in the small plastic tray, the first of many you will see. In fact, the small plastic tray might as well be the cultural ambassador of Japan. You will rarely hand your money or credit card directly to anyone; you'll place it in the tray, then they'll put your change and receipt in it and hand it back to you. Very presentational. Very formal. Very Japanese.

CASH FRIENDLY:
TO USE YOUR ATM CARD, YOU NEED TO FIND AN "INTERNATIONAL" ATM. THEY ARE DENOTED BY THIS "POSTAL" SYMBOL.

ATMS
These are a little tricky, because local ATMs and even banks won't work with your ATM card. A bank can give you a cash advance, but you have to set that up ahead of time. Additionally, traveler's checks need to be cashed by a bank or hotel. To use your ATM card, you need to find an "international" ATM, denoted by the "postal" symbol shown at right. They are not very common, so all foreign expatriates know where they are. They usually allow a maximum daily cash withdrawal of 50,000 yen.

CREDIT CARDS
Assuming you have heeded our advice and called your credit card provider before traveling overseas, credit cards seem to work fine everywhere. One interesting note is that people in Japan rarely carry debt, so you might be asked if you would like a larger transaction to be divided into phases. What this means is that for a fee, the Tokyo merchant will spread your purchase price out over multiple billing cycles. This service is not typically preapproved for international credit cards, so we recommend avoiding it, no matter how desperate you are for an expensive item. Finally, just to make things sporty, there is a good chance that your card will be deactivated while you are in Tokyo. We know you called before you left, just like we told you to, but sometimes it happens anyway. If it does, don't panic. Take it in stride, call the credit card company at your next convenience, and use a different card if you have one.

THE TRAY:
LIKE A SMALL PLASTIC SHADOW, THIS TRAY WILL FOLLOW YOU EVERYWHERE YOU GO. DON'T FIGHT THE TRAY. THE TRAY HAS FRIENDS. LOTS OF THEM.

JAPANESE CURRENCY IS CALLED YEN. THE EASIEST WAY TO THINK OF IT IS THAT ONE YEN IS THE SAME AS ONE PENNY. THAT MEANS 100 YEN ARE LIKE 100 PENNIES. IF YOU WANT TO THINK OF YEN AS DOLLARS, SIMPLY INSERT A DECIMAL POINT BEFORE THE LAST TWO DIGITS IN THE NUMBER, SO 100 YEN ARE THE EQUIVALENT OF $1.00.

DOLLARS TO YEN EXCHANGE RATE

	85 ¥	90 ¥	95 ¥	100 ¥	105 ¥	110 ¥
1,000 ¥	$11.50	$11	$10.50	$10	$9.50	$9
5,000 ¥	$57.50	$55	$52.50	$50	$47.50	$45
10,000 ¥	$115	$110	$105	$100	$95	$90
50,000 ¥	$575	$550	$525	$500	$475	$450
100,000 ¥	$1150	$1100	$1050	$1000	$950	$900
Amount in Yen						Amount in USD

EXCHANGE RATE
To figure out your currency exchange rate, the easiest way to think of it is to assume that every number above 100 yen equals that percentage off the price. Therefore, a 110 yen exchange rate means you get 10 percent off the price, or $ 0.90. For an exchange under 100, every yen means that you should add it on to the price. A 90 yen exchange rate is 10 yen less than 100, so you need to add 10 to the price, or $1.10. It may sound confusing at first, but it will become easy once you do it a few times.

1 YEN
THE JAPANESE VERSION OF A PENNY. THESE ARE COMPLETELY WORTHLESS, AND THEY FEEL LIKE IT. THEY MAY ACTUALLY BE MINTED OUT OF AIR. SILVER, LIGHT, AND SMALL, THEY WILL PILE UP LIKE USELESS TOKENS.

10 YEN
SIMILAR TO A DIME, BUT DECENT SIZE, BROWN, AND EVERYWHERE. EVERY TIME YOU REACH INTO YOUR POCKET, YOU WILL FIND A MILLION OF THESE. GOOD FOR TRAINS AND NOT MUCH ELSE.

5 YEN
THE NICKEL OF JAPAN. ANOTHER WORTHLESS COIN. SO WORTHLESS, IN FACT, THAT THEY DID NOT EVEN BOTHER TO PUT A NUMBER ON IT. (OR MAYBE THEY DID THAT JUST TO CONFUSE THE TOURISTS.) REGARDLESS, YOU CAN'T USE IT FOR TRAIN FARE. LUCKILY, EVERYONE LIKES TO ROUND RETAIL PRICES TO THE FIVE YEN, SO YOU CAN GET RID OF IT THEN.

50 YEN
A TRICKY LITTLE COIN, AND SMALLER THAN EVERY OTHER COIN EXCEPT THE 1 YEN, THE 50 YEN COIN IS SILVER AND HAS A HOLE IN THE CENTER. THIS IS THE COIN PEOPLE KEEP AS A SOUVENIR SO THEY CAN TELL THEIR FRIENDS, "LOOK, IT HAS A HOLE IN THE CENTER." (THEY ALSO WON'T TAKE IT AT THE MONEY EXCHANGE, SO YOU END UP WITH A SOUVENIR WHETHER YOU LIKE IT OR NOT.)

500 YEN
THE BIG JERK OF THE COIN WORLD, THIS OVERSIZE GOLD BRICK WEIGHS A TON. WITHIN THE FIRST DAY, YOU WILL BE DITCHING THESE EVERYWHERE OR PAYING FOR YOUR WHOLE GROUP'S TRAIN FARE WITH THEM. TOO EXPENSIVE TO IGNORE, AND TOO BIG TO LOVE.

100 YEN
A MUCH HEAVIER, SILVER COIN, THIS IS JUST SLIGHTLY SMALLER THAN A QUARTER, MUCH THICKER, AND WORTH FOUR TIMES AS MUCH. THINK OF IT AS A SILVER DOLLAR. THESE WILL ADD UP QUICK, AND BEFORE YOU KNOW IT, YOU WILL HAVE 2,000 YEN IN CHANGE. GOOD THING YOU CAN EXCHANGE THESE.

1,000 YEN
YOUR FIRST BILL, ONE OF THESE EQUALS A WHOLE POCKET OF HEAVY CHANGE, SO ONLY BREAK ONE IF IT'S ABSOLUTELY NECESSARY.

10,000 YEN
THE BIG BILL, THIS ONE CAN TRICK YOU, SO ALWAYS COUNT THE ZEROS. DON'T MISTAKE THIS FOR 1,000 YEN, OR VICE VERSA. FATTEN UP YOUR WALLET WITH A PILE OF THEM AND GET READY FOR A DAY OF SHOPPING.

5,000 YEN
THE MIDDLE CHILD OF THE BILL FAMILY. QUIET, UNASSUMING, AND PLEASANT. THERE IS NOT MUCH MORE TO SAY ABOUT THIS BILL.

WHERE DO I GO FROM HERE?
We don't know where you're headed, so we can't tell you how to get there. Before you panic, though, here are a few common options that will probably work.

LIMOUSINE BUS: Probably the cheapest option from the airport, the bus counter is located right across from your exit from customs. The limousine bus travels from Narita Airport to all major city areas and hotels. They usually run every hour to ninety minutes, so you can always wait for the next one if you miss your bus. It generally costs about 3,000 yen per person and is a very comfortable ride. For more details, you can look them up on the web at: www.limousinebus.co.jp/e/index_route.html.

CAB: Cabs are available, but are very expensive.

CAR SERVICE: This is even more expensive than a cab. Then again, if you are considering this option, you probably flew first class anyway.

TRAIN: We usually end up taking the Narita Express. It runs all the time and costs 3,000–4,000 yen for a ticket, depending on your final destination. To get there, take the escalators downstairs. The hallways open up into an area with shops and a Starbucks. This is the right place. The Narita Express ticket counter is located in the back right of this area. It heads to eight major neighborhoods in Tokyo, including Shinjuku and Shibuya. By riding the Narita Express instead of the limousine bus, you get to see the scenery instead of the highway, and who knew the airport was so far away from the city? If you take the Narita Express, you can transfer to most other train lines at its major stops.

WHERE TO STAY
Oh, man, we wouldn't touch this one with a ten-foot pole. Use the Internet. Find out what is where, and how much you want to spend. We would suggest staying "central," so getting around is easy. We recommend Shibuya, as there is always something to do there, as well as Shinjuku, but there are lots of other places to stay. Staying in Roppongi is also popular, and anything on the JR Yamanote line is helpful. Because you have so many options, we'll leave it up to you to figure out your hotel on your own.

TRANSPORTATION
Now that you are in Tokyo, you have dropped off your luggage and are itching to get around. The easiest way to do so is by train. There are three kinds of trains: the JR system, the Tokyo Metro Subway, and private train lines. Before you panic, you don't really need to know most of it. Everything in this book is based on the main JR system, and of all the lines on the JR map, you really only need two: the JR Yamanote and the JR Sobu.

Really, it's that simple. There are two trains: one that goes in a circle, one that follows a straight line. The Yamanote is always highlighted by a green line, and is one of the most popular train lines in Tokyo. It is easy to get to, and the trains show up every four minutes like clockwork. The Sobu line is a bit more local and runs in two forms: local (all stops) in yellow, and express (big stops only) in orange. For starters, ignore the orange express, and look only for the local yellow, which will get you everywhere you need to go. After you get comfortable with your new train, you can graduate to other train lines, but for now, keep it simple, and you will be just fine.

YOUR FIRST TRAIN RIDE:
THE NARITA EXPRESS MAKES EIGHT STOPS THROUGHOUT TOKYO. THE TRAIN RIDE TO SHIBUYA/SHINJUKU IS ALMOST ONE HOUR FROM NARITA AIRPORT.

- NARITA AIRPORT
- YOTSUKAIDO
- CHIBA
- TOKYO
- SHINAGAWA
- SHIBUYA
- SHINJUKU
- IKEBUKURO
- OMIYA

81

011 + 81 + 3 + TEL#
- US TO TOKYO -

☎

01

01 + 1 + AREA CODE + TEL#
001 + 1 + AREA CODE + TEL#
- TOKYO TO US -

GETTING AROUND
Train stations are labeled in both English and Japanese on alternating signs, so anywhere along the way, you can check the station names. The super-fancy Yamanote line even has LEDs with the stop names, digital maps, and voice-overs telling you everything you need to know, as well as occasional English lessons. Trust us, it's almost too easy on the Yamanote.

HOW TO PAY FOR A FARE
Fares are based on the distance you are traveling. The minimum fare on all the JR train lines is 140 yen. To figure out how much you need to pay, consult the diagram in the train station. The bigger stations usually have an English version; some smaller local stations are only in Japanese, but you can count your stops from the diagram and figure out the price. If you are wrong, it's easy to correct the price at your destination. Just look for the circle (Yamanote) and the line through it (Sobu) on the diagram, and you will know where you are like a seasoned local.

SUICA CARDS
A preferred method of payment by many travelers who are not buying rail passes, a Suica card is a rechargeable debit card that allows you to pay for train fare on all train lines. Additionally, the Suica card can be used at many vending machines and even some shops, making it a convenient alternative to a pocketful of change if you are so inclined. The initial charge for a Suica card is 2,000 yen, and it can be purchased at nearly any train station.

TIME CHANGES
Tokyo is across the International Date Line from the United States, so it is one day ahead. If it is Friday in the States, it is Saturday in Tokyo. Toyko is eight hours behind the West Coast, or eleven hours behind the East Coast. This is always a little confusing, so we made you a handy chart.

TOKYO	HONOLULU	WEST COAST	MOUNTAIN	CENTRAL	EAST COAST
NOON SATURDAY	5 PM FRIDAY	8 PM FRIDAY	9 PM FRIDAY	10 PM FRIDAY	11 PM FRIDAY

MAKING A PHONE CALL
If you are calling into Tokyo, the country code is 81 and the city code is 3. Therefore, to dial Tokyo, you need to dial 011+81+3+(telephone number). If you are calling from Tokyo to the United States, the country code is 01. So, to dial back across the ocean, you need to dial 01+1+[area code]+[telephone number]. In some places, you will need to dial 001+1+[area code]+[telephone number], based on varying phone providers.

CELL PHONES
As Japan has its own specific cell phone network, only a handful of cell phones are compatible with its system. The minimum for your phone should be 3G compatible, and a fairly recent 3G at that. Most cell phone providers require you to setup and activate your international plan no fewer than ten days before your departure, or your phone bill may be more than the cost of the phone itself. Many hotels also offer rental phones while you are in town, but check the rates ahead of time. Many plans are affordable, but some can be quite pricey.

BACKUP PLAN:
BE EQUIPPED WITH YOUR HOTEL AND EMERGENCY NUMBERS AND PASSPORT INFORMATION, SO YOU'LL HAVE AN OUT IF ANYTHING HAPPENS. HOPEFULLY YOU WILL NEVER NEED THIS INFORMATION. SO PUT IT IN YOUR WALLET AND FORGET IT'S EVEN THERE.

BATHROOMS

Public restrooms are few and far between, so restaurants and department stores are your best bet. Most toilets have a dizzying array of buttons and functions that we have never figured out. What we do know is this: The toilets make noise or swirl water to help cover your "natural sounds," and one of those side buttons shoots precisely aimed water lasers, so watch out. If you end up at a public restroom out of desperation, you will be faced with a prehistoric squat toilet. Be sure to grab some of the giveaway tissues before heading in, as there is no paper or towels for wiping or drying.

SHIPPING

If you have bought so much that you need to ship it home, there are a few options for you. UPS and FedEx work if you have your own account already, and the Japanese postal system offers two forms of international shipping: Surface/Air/Land (SAL) and Express Mail Service (EMS). SAL is generally cheaper, but it has a maximum size you cannot exceed, and the packages take anywhere from five days to four weeks to arrive. EMS (Express Mail Service) is more expensive, but you can send much larger items than you can through SAL, and packages are automatically insured and arrive in just three days. Ultimately, finding a post office to mail these items from can be a pain, but your hotel can usually prearrange an EMS pickup from most locations.

A HELPING HAND: YAMATO DELIVERS EVERYWHERE THAT YOU DON'T WANT TO, QUICKLY AND INEXPENSIVELY. YOU WILL SEE THE YAMATO CAT LOGO ALL OVER TOWN. ISN'T THAT CUTE.

YAMATO SERVICE

You probably won't need this, but this is the greatest thing ever. Someone needs to bring this service to the United States. Yamato is a glorified courier service that allows you to deliver shipments within the city of Tokyo. For a very small fee, you can send unwieldy boxes or other items to your hotel or friend's house. Yamato delivers twenty-four hours a day, so you can pick your drop-off time in six-hour windows to guarantee that someone is available to receive your box when it is delivered. You will see the cat logo all over Tokyo. These guys deserve a medal.

LOCKERS

If you are running around and need to stash your loot for later, most train stations have lockers that rent for 100–600 yen, depending on the size of the locker. Drop off your stuff here and keep shopping; just make sure to come back and get it.

VENDING MACHINES

These are everywhere, and sell almost everything you could want. Some of the teas and coffees are even designed to heat up once opened. If you ever need anything to drink or snack on, these are lifesavers, and the only things open at 6:00 AM.

TIPPING

Gratuity is always included, whether in a restaurant, a cab, or a hotel. Most people will not accept a tip even if you insist, and some will even be annoyed at the concept. Keep the change, because they won't.

TRASH
There are very few trash cans, so expect to carry your trash with you until you find one. There is usually a trash can at most vending machine groups, as well as at the entrances to convenience stores. You won't see any litter, so don't start a trend—take your trash with you.

JAYWALKING
Almost everyone waits for the light to cross the street in major areas, and uses the crosswalks. In residential areas, rules are much more lax, but expect to wait with the masses when you are around town.

SLEEPING
When you arrive in Tokyo, stay up as late as you possibly can. The later you stay up, the later you will be able to sleep in the morning. Once you go to bed, sleep for as long as you can. Toss, turn, roll over, and do whatever you can to keep your eyes shut. When you finally give up on sleeping, take a look at the clock. It will be 6:00 AM. We guarantee it.

WHAT TO DO AT 6:00 AM
In all honesty, there isn't a lot to do this early in the morning. Almost nothing is open—no shops, very few restaurants, and a handful of convenience stores (and that bookstore in Shibuya, but more on that later). So grab a snack, take a train ride, visit a temple, go for a jog, do Sudoku, call home . . . basically, keep yourself occupied until 10:00 or 11:00 AM, when shops will start to open.

SMOKING:
ONCE A NATIONAL PASTIME, SMOKING HAS BEEN SEVERELY CURTAILED IN THE LAST FEW YEARS, AND IS NO LONGER ALLOWED IN MANY PUBLIC AREAS OR MANY RESTAURANTS. FOR SOME OF YOU, THIS WILL BE AN UNWELCOME CHANGE, BUT FOR THE REST OF US, IT ALLOWS US TO FINALLY COME BACK FROM OVERSEAS NOT SMELLING LIKE A FACTORY.

Now that all that is behind us, let's move on to the good stuff. On the following pages are maps to different neighborhoods in Tokyo. Each map features the best stores, with dark green flags designating "highlighted shops," and light green flags indicating "secondary shops." Points of interest and other shops are shown with a light brown flag, with visual landmarks marked in gray. Last, the Koban, or neighborhood police boxes, are shown with blue hats. If you get lost or need anything, stop by the Koban. It's like a neighborhood information box that just happens to be staffed by policemen.

So get out there and have a good time. Wander down side streets, poke your head into tiny shops, and relax. Although Tokyo is a city that never ends, you are never far from a train that can get you back to wherever you came from. Now get going—you didn't fly all the way over here just to read this book, did you?

GREETINGS
Ohayou ....Good morning
Konnichiwa ....Good afternoon
Konbanwa ....Good evening
Oyasumi ....Good night
Sayonara ....Goodbye
Moshi Moshi ....Hello (on the phone)

TALK THE TALK
In a surprising coincidence, everyone in Tokyo speaks Japanese. Some people speak a little English and are more than happy to try to work it out while you butcher their language. If someone knows English, they are more likely able to read and write it than speak it, so have a notebook handy. In the interest of fair play, here are a few key phrases you can use to impress your new Japanese friends.

TOY SHOPPING LINGO
Kaiju ....Monster
Chogokin ....Die-cast robots
Sofubi ....Soft vinyl
Sentai ....Team series TV shows
Otaku ....Fans of anime, manga, and video games
Kore katte kureru? ....Will you buy this for me?
(Kore wa) ikura desa ka? ....How much?

HELPFUL PHRASES
Hai ....Yes
Ie ....No
Tabun ....Maybe
Tasukete! ....Help
Domo ....Thanks (informal)
Arigatou ....Thanks (informal)
Domo Arigatou ....Thank you very much (formal)
Sumimasen ....Excuse me/Pardon me
O namae wa nan desu ka? ....What is your name?
Onegai ....Please
Mayotte shimai mashita ....I'm lost
Gomen nasai ....I'm sorry
Su goi! ....Cool
Eigo wo hanashi masu ka? ....Do you speak English?
_____ ni wa dou ikebaii desu ka? ....How do I get to _____
Kono densha wa _____ ni tomari masu ka? ....Does this train stop at _____
Toire wa doko desu ka? ....Where is the bathroom?

TOKYO NEIGHBORHOODS

SHIBUYA
HARAJUKU/AOYAMA
SHINJUKU
NAKANO
KOENJI
KICHIJOJI
AKIHABARA
KOIWA/KAMEIDO
EBISU/DAIKANYAMA
SHIMOKITAZAWA

JR EAST RAILWAY LINES IN GREATER TOKYO

For your introduction to Tokyo, here is the map to the JR train system. Don't worry, though; you don't need to know all this. Just turn the page, and we will make it easier for you. Visit www.jreast.co.jp for more information.

NISHI-NIPPORI

EKODA

IKEBUKURO

KICHIJOJI　　NAKANO　　SHINJUKU

KOENJI

HARAJUKU

SHIMO KITAZAWA

SHIBUYA

EBISU

TRANSIT

Feel free to ignore that giant map on the preceding pages. The only two trains you really need (for this book, at least) are the JR Yamanote (green) and the JR Sobu (yellow). The other six train lines shown here are for trips to single, specific neighborhoods, and you will use them only once.

It's easy to get around town. The JR Yamanote goes in a circle, so you can always get back to where you came from. The JR Sobu is a straight west-to-east line that can drop you off inside or outside the Yamanote circle.

Now then, that wasn't so scary after all, was it?

AOTO

MACHIYA

AKIHABARA

KAMEIDO

KOIWA

BIG SIGHT

SHIMBASHI

JR SYSTEM	OTHER TRAIN LINES	
YAMANOTE	CHIYODA	KEIO INOKASHIRA
SŌBU LOCAL	SEIBU-IKEBUKURO	YURIKAMOME MONORAIL
	KEISEI	

- **HIGHLIGHT SHOPS**
- **SECONDARY SHOPS**
- **POINTS OF INTEREST**
- **LANDMARKS**
- **KOBAN POLICE**
- **YAMANOTE**
- **SŌBU LOCAL**

TRUE

17

TOKYU DEPT. STORE

SHIBUYA

One of Tokyo's most famous shopping districts, Shibuya is a must-stop for any traveler. Most famous for its two-minute crosswalk, as seen in movies like *Lost in Translation*, it is one of the most photographed locations in the entire city. With abundant hotels and access from the JR Yamanote line, Tokyo Metro Subway system, and Keio train lines, Shibuya never sleeps. Anchored by large department stores Parco, 0101, Tokyu, and variety store Tokyu Hands, its streets are littered with boutiques large and small, offering a little something for everyone.

01_ HACHIKO DOG STATUE 02_ 24-HOUR BOOKSTORE 03_ DON QUIXOTE 04_ CITIBANK ATM 05_ RAJ 06_ DISC UNION
07_ CURRY PLAZA 08_ MANDARAKE 09_ TOYKU HANDS 10_ PARCO 3 11_ PARCO 1 12_ PARCO 2 13_ GRANIPH
14_ TOWER RECORDS 15_ BAPE 16_ LA SOFFITTA PIZZERIA 17_ PROJECT 1/6 18_ NHK STUDIOS

MOS BURGER

GIANT NECK FACE ERAS

ATM

KFC

PACHINKO TOWER
SOFT BANK

TV
GIANT CROSS WALK
TV

TO HARAJUKU

HACHIKO EXIT
JR SHIBUYA STATION

KEIO SHIBUYA STATION
TO DAIKANYAMA

SHIBUYA

Shibuya is a great place to start your trip, as it offers you a taste of every stereotype you could hope to see in Tokyo.

If you are coming from the JR train station, look for signs leading you to the Hachiko exit at the north end of the station. As is true in most Tokyo train stations, you will see myriad exits, but Hachiko is the only one you need. As you exit the train station, the Koban (police box) will be on your right, and a crush of people will be in front of you. Across the plaza is a statue of Hachiko (01) and a newly installed smoking area. Once you get your bearings, look for the giant television screens. The bigger of the two should be directly across the intersection, above the Starbucks. See, it's just like home. When the red lights come on and the walk sign lights up, you have the next two minutes to get across. All directions head at once, so, like a salmon swimming upstream, make your way to any side you choose.

A conveniently located ATM is not far from the Shibuya station, so if you need to get some quick cash, this is a perfect time. Just past the McDonald's on the left is Citibank (04). If you ever feel a little lost and need to see another Western face, just wait here for a minute, and you're bound to see an expatriate popping out of the woodwork for a quick cash withdrawal. Just next door is discount wonderland Don Quixote (03), a late-night closeout shop of confounding and confusing, yet somewhat charming, variety.

For toy shops, Mandarake Shibuya (08) and Project 1/6 (17) are the only shops in the area. To complete all your travel stories, you should plan a trip to hardware superstore Tokyu Hands (09), where you can find everything that you never knew you needed.

After loading up on gifts, turn your attention to Parco 1 (11), 2 (12), and 3 (10). These three stores represent the best of boutique shopping in a department store setting. The Logos and Libro bookstores in the bottom of Parco 1 are our favorite bookstores in the city. The Tower bookstore (14), on the seventh floor of Tower Records, is a close second. Tower also sells CDs and, unlike their American counterpart, is still in business and has everything you're looking for. Design and magazine junkies will find the twenty-four-hour bookstore (02) worth checking out as well.

Not far from Tower is designer-t-shirt shop Graniph (13), selling affordable tees in constantly updated styles. Every American we know has become addicted to their "two tees for 4,500 yen" deal, a gateway drug to fabric crack. Along the way, keep your eyes peeled for a GIANT, Neck Face, and ERAS art piece that has been quietly occupying wall space just off the street for years now. For more high-dollar threads, head over to the new Bape (15) flagship store and get your street-fashion cred straight from the source.

For quick eats or an early dinner, there are a couple of places you should try and many you should avoid (Shakey's, we're looking at you). If you like Indian, Curry Plaza (07) is easy to find, located between Tokyu Hands and Mandarake, while RAJ (05) is the neighborhood secret, squeezed in between a few floors of less reputable establishments. La Soffitta (16) is an Italian dinnertime staple on every Super7 trip, and provides one English-language menu for your entire group of diners.

Other shops include Disc Union (06), which has a great punk record store on the fifth floor, and, at the opposite end of Shibuya, NHK Studios (18). For those of you familiar with Domokun, there is a gift store in the basement of NHK Studios that is the only place in Tokyo where you can still get Domokun items with any regularity.

From NHK, a short stroll past the stadium will lead you to Harajuku, if you are up for a leisurely walk. Otherwise, head back to the train station and proceed to the next stop.

DOMOKUN:
THE FURRY, CHOCOLATE-COLORED WALL OF TEETH WAS THE TELEVISION STATION NHK'S MASCOT UNTIL JUST RECENTLY. THE ONLY WORD HE CAN SPEAK IS "DOMO," WHICH HE SAYS IN A MILLION DIFFERENT WAYS TO INDICATE EVERY NEED OR EMOTION. HE LOVES TELEVISION, HIS FAVORITE BAND IS GUITAR WOLF, AND WHEN HE GETS NERVOUS, HE PASSES GAS.

08

MANDARAKE
B2 31-2 UDAGAWACHO, SHIBUYA-KU
03-3477-0777, WWW.MANDARAKE.CO.JP/ENGLISH/SHOP/SBY.HTML
HOURS: 12:00 — 20:00

Easily the best-known toy shop in Japan, Mandarake is actually a chain of stores with shops spread all over the country. Mandarake specializes in secondhand goods, and the stock changes on literally a daily basis. The Shibuya Mandarake is no exception. Down two flights of stairs, covered in cavelike stucco and lit with seizure-inducing blinking lights, the store's descent is part of every visitor's tales of the city. Once you have safely arrived in the second-floor basement, there are rows and rows of manga, video games, mini-erasers, and, of course, toys. From vintage 1950s Tezuka *Astroboy* issues and original Marusan figures all the way up to last week's Bandai release or *Shonen Jump* issue, Mandarake has a plethora of items to choose from, usually at some of the best prices in the city. A must-stop for any traveler, just to marvel at the overwhelming nature of it all, or to buy some really great stuff you won't find anywhere else.

SHIBUYA

HACHIKO 01

The legend of Hachiko is amazing and depressing at the same time. The story goes that every day, a professor, Ueno Eizaburo, would walk with his dog, Hachiko, to the train station and go to work. Hachiko would then meet him at the end of the day to walk home together. One day, while at work, the professor had a heart attack and died. That day, Hachiko waited for the professor to come home on the train, which he never did. Hachiko returned to the train station, waiting for the professor to come home, every day for the rest of his life. Hachiko died nearly ten years later, along the way becoming a national hero for his loyalty and perseverance.

BAPE 15
RISE BLDG, 13-17 UDAGAWA-CHO, SHIBUYA-KU
03-6415-6041, WWW.BAPE.COM
HOURS: 11:00 — 19:00

A newcomer to Shibuya, the newest Bape boutique features a moving treadmill hiding underneath the glass floor, as well as more t-shirts, shoes, and other gear than you can shake your wallet at. Hipsters line up early in the morning. and there is a limit to the amount of people allowed in the store at any given time, so make sure you have a few minutes to spare before heading over.

43

10, 11, 12

PARCO 1, 2, 3
15-1 UDAGAWA, SHIBUYA-KU
03-3464-5111, WWW.PARCO-SHIBUYA.COM
HOURS: 10:00 — 21:00

Shibuya's Parco department store is actually three entire buildings. Known as Parco 1, Parco 2, and Parco 3, this department store puts most others to shame within minutes. While most floors are devoted to the latest in boutique fashion, the basement of Parco 1 is home to Delfonics, the Logos and Libro bookstores, a small gallery, and a few other specialty shops. Time and time again, this bottom floor is full of books and design goods that exist seemingly nowhere else on Earth. The café on the ground floor has good snack food for a quick bite, but falls short for a meal. The second floor of Parco 2 is home to housewares company Franc Franc, and well worth a stop if you are even remotely interested in stylish furnishings. Additionally, the basement level of Parco 3 features a constant rotation of new and interesting shops, while the seventh floor is home to a massive gallery that usually has world-class, can't-miss art shows.

9
TOKYU HANDS
12-18 UDAGAWACHO, SHIBUYA-KU
03-5489-5111, WWW.TOKYU-HANDS.CO.JP/SHIBUYA.HTM
HOURS: 10:00 — 20:30

Rarely would anyone recommend a hardware store as a necessary stop, but Japan's Tokyu Hands is the exception to that rule. Stacked to the ceiling on eight staircase-filled floors (each featuring three sublevels), this retailer specializes in the unexpected. From stickers and stationery to trash cans and household appliances, from study aids and luggage to lumber and candy toys, you never know what you will find at this all-encompassing retailer. Affordably priced and showcasing the most extreme product juxtapositions from floor to floor, Tokyu Hands provides every traveler with a good story to share.

17
PROJECT 1/6
37-10 UDAGAWA, SHIBUYA-KU
03-3467-7676, WWW.MEDICOMTOY.CO.JP/INDEX_SHOPINFO.HTML

While not everyone may be familiar with the name Medicom, you probably know their products. Most famous for their ever-expanding line of Kubrick and Be@rbrick miniature figures, Medicom has been a toy staple in Japan for over a decade. Medicom originally began manufacturing hyper-detailed twelve-inch figures of comic, movie, and television characters, and has exploded ever since, becoming one of Japan's leading toy manufacturers. Project 1/6 is Medicom's flagship store, named after the scale ratio of their original twelve-inch figures. Nestled just off the main streets of Shibuya, it is worth dropping into to see the latest in Medicom goods, or any new store exclusives.

- HIGHLIGHT SHOPS
- SECONDARY SHOPS
- POINTS OF INTEREST
- LANDMARKS
- KOBAN POLICE
- YAMANOTE
- SŌBU LOCAL

HARAJUKU STATION

TO TEMPLE

STADIUM

TAKESHITA ALLEY

MEIJI-DORI STREET

TO SHIBUYA

HARAJUKU

Yet another of Tokyo's signature neighborhoods, Harajuku is best known for being both the birthplace and the cutting edge of current Japanese street fashion and culture. Weekends you'll see tiny shops with lines wrapped around the block for the latest shoe, denim, clothing, or toy release. Sundays are especially dramatic, with gothic Lolitas, 1950s rockabilly hounds, and homemade fashionistas dressing up to full effect and posing for pictures at the south end of the JR Yamanote Harajuku station.

01_ SUNDAY GOTH GIRL CRAZINESS 02_ ROCKABILLY DUDES 03_ MUJI 04_ PIZZA EXPRESS RESTAURANT 05_ BLISTER 06_ ICE CREAM 07_ KINETICS 08_ ATMOS 09_ (UT) UNIQLO TEE 10_ NEIGHBORHOOD 11_ STÜSSY BONEYARD 12_ UNDEFEATED 13_ GRANIPH 14_ SPIRAL TOY SHOP 15_ BEAMS TEE 16_ BAPE CAFÉ 17_ BAPE KIDS 18_ BAPE CUTS 19_ NIKE AFI 25TH ANNIVERSARY 20_ BOUNTY HUNTER 21_ EROSTIKA 22_ SECRET BASE 23_ SUPREME 24_ MADFOOT 25_ GRAVIS/REAL MAD HECTIC 26_ XLARGE/XGIRL 27_ INVISIBLE MAN 28_ AIRSTREAM BURGER 29_ KIDDYLAND 30_ ATROMIKE 31_ KUA 'AINA BURGER 32_ HYSTERIC GLAMOUR FLAGSHIP STORE 33_ PRADA 34_ BAPE FLAGSHIP STORE 35_ MIU MIU 36_ ORIGINAL FAKE 37_ DOVER STREET MARKET 38_ GOOD DESIGN 39_ BLACK FLAG CORSO COMO 40_ REED SPACE 41_ MISHKA

AOYAMA

Less traveled by tourists, but just as vibrant, is the more upscale Aoyama. Considered to be a more grown-up version of Harajuku, high fashion and luxury goods mix with streetwear and lifestyle stores on every street. While Harajuku is accessible from both the JR Yamanote line and the Chiyoda Metro Subway system, Aoyama is not. That said, it is an easy five-minute walk east from Harajuku.

22
SECRET BASE
3-15-8-#205 JINGUUMAE, SHIBUYA-KU
03-3403-8188, WWW.SECRET-B.COM
HOURS: 12:00 — 20:00

Just off to the side of Harajuku, upstairs and to the left, lies Secret Base, one of Japan's better-known manufacturers of modern vinyl. In a new location at the northern end of Harajuku, and with more than three hundred figure releases under its belt—as well as collaborations with Balzac, Pushead, Super7, Usugrow, Hiro-Grim, Saga-Chan, and Take-Shit, to name a few—this toy boutique has a loyal, almost cultish following. With new releases nearly every two weeks, chances are good that some limited figure will be available at any given moment. In spite of its relentless schedule, Secret Base remains in high demand, and most releases sell out quickly.

What can be said about Harajuku that hasn't been said before? Heck, even Gwen Stefani names songs and her backup dancers after these cool kids. To see Harajuku at its absolute craziest, stop by on a Sunday. At the south end of the station (01), the finest in homemade fashion will be on parade and ready for pictures. Dominated by gothic Lolitas and immortalized in books like *Fruits*, this Sunday afternoon fashion show puts Paris on notice and makes you wonder what these kids do for the rest of the week. Just across the bridge, at the entrance to the park, will be groups of retro rockabilly dudes (02) in full gear, dancing the afternoon away. Is it crazier that we are mentioning it or that they are dead serious?

From one fashion extreme to another, head on over to Harajuku proper. Home to the latest in hipster streetwear from around the globe, and every type of sneaker imaginable, Harajuku is not for those with a light wallet or well-worn shoes. Some of the best local shops and brands, sure to bump up your street cred, are Kinetics (07), Neighborhood (10), Madfoot (24), Real Mad Hectic (25), and Invisible Man (27), as well as American brands XLarge and X-girl (26), Stüssy (11), Undefeated (12), Supreme (23), Mishka (41), and the Nike twenty-fifth anniversary Air Force 1 shop (19).

For art lovers, we suggest stopping by the Real Mad Hectic shop (25) to see a large group of Phil Frost paintings, and the Bape Café (16) to see the original paintings of KAWS' *Kimpsons* preserved for eternity. Speaking of Bape, the worldwide domination of *Planet of the Apes* iconography has extended to both a kids' store (17) and a barbershop (18) located nearby, which have to be seen to be believed (who can imagine a playpen full of foam bananas?).

On the outermost edge of Harajuku is punk rock fashion house Bounty Hunter (20). Known for its clothes and toys, it is a destination for punks and toy nerds alike. Located just behind Bounty Hunter, around the corner and up a flight of stairs, is artist Rockin' Jellybean's shop, Erostika (21), stocked full of prints, clothing, and everything else you may need for your inner hot rod. Across the hall is Secret Base (22), one of Tokyo's most sought-after manufacturers of soft-vinyl kaiju, and frequent collaborator with Usugrow, Pushead, and Super7.

Back on the main street, Omoto-Sando, and on the other side of the bridge is the multiple-story new toy paradise known as Kiddy Land (29). Though it caters more to little ladies than to boys, Kiddy Land still has a bit of everything. For the toy-shop completist, a quick trip down the side alleys will take you to Astro Mike (30), a shop specializing in newer, more affordable toys and knickknacks. Along the way, stop in at the small Muji (03) for a quick take on their beautiful but simple and utilitarian approach to everyday items, toy shop Spiral (14) for a cacophonous mix of old and new character goods, or the world-famous action-figure heaven Blister (05).

AOYAMA

Just a short walk from Harajuku is the more upscale Aoyama. There, luxury brands rub shoulders with the streetwear elite and a few brands that manage to straddle the line.

For designer-toy hunters, the main point of a trip to Aoyama is to see the impressive Original Fake (36). With its giant anatomical study of the KAWS Companion guarding the entrance, KAWS' flagship store has housed almost every new KAWS release since its opening. Equally impressive in design, and worth seeing even if you care nothing for the brands, are Miu Miu (35), the Bape flagship store (34), the Hysteric Glamour flagship store (32), and Prada (33). Other shops worth browsing are Staple's Reed Space (just behind Marc Jacobs, and just off the map (40)), Black Flag (39), Dover Street (37), and, for the modernists houseware-and-furniture lover in you, Good Design (38). After all that walking, head over to Kua 'Aina (31) for a great burger or veggie sandwich direct from Hawaii, return to Harajuku for a burger at the Airstream trailer (28), or go one floor above the Gap for pizza and pasta from London's Pizza Express (04).

WRITING ON THE WALL:
BEST KNOWN FOR HIS CLEAN, WAVY LINE WORK, KAMI'S ALTER EGO PAINTS THESE LITTLE SHAPES ALL AROUND THE CITY. WHEN YOU SEE ONE, YOU KNOW THAT "KAMI WAS HERE," JUST LIKE YOU ARE. THEN YOU CAN TELL YOUR FRIENDS YOU CROSSED PATHS WITH ONE OF TOKYO'S FINEST ARTISTS.

16
BAPE CAFÉ
3-27-22 JINGUMAE, SHIBUYA-KU
03-5770-6560
HOURS: 10:30 — 20:00

While not an official retail store, the Bape Café is an easy place to grab a quick drink or snack while jetting around Harajuku. The real reason for its mention is not the food, but the artwork lining the walls. The entire bottom floor is ringed with the original KAWS *Kimpsons* paintings in perfect, single scale, with no character left unturned. For good measure, the giant *Kimpsons* Sergeant Pepper homage is the centerpiece of the second floor. This is a must-see for any KAWS or modern-vinyl fan.

20
BOUNTY HUNTER
3-15-8 JINGUMAE, SHIBUYA-KU
3-3746-1044, WWW.BOUNTY-HUNTER.COM
HOURS: 12:00 — 20:00

Renowned as one of the innovators of Japanese punk rock street fashion, and considered one of the original vinyl toy manufacturers, Bounty Hunter has set countless trends that others try to follow. After releasing their genre-inducing Kid Hunter figure in 1999, Bounty Hunter was the first toy company to work with now-ingrained toy designers KAWS, Frank Kozik, and James Jarvis, while creating their own signature character, the Skull Kun. Named after founder Hikaru Iwanaga's obsession with the Star Wars bounty hunter Boba Fett, Bounty Hunter is always unafraid to do the unexpected. People go for the fashion, but Bounty Hunter's biggest claim to fame may be the toy movement it helped inspire.

SPIRAL TOY SHOP   **14**
A-1 NAGATA BLDG, 3-27-17 JINGUMAE, SHIBUYA-KU
03-3479-1262, WWW.SPIRAL-TOY.COM
HOURS: 12:00 — 20:30

A small shop tucked out of the way and across from Secret Base, Spiral's newer toys and characters span a broad spectrum. Focusing more on lines like The Nightmare Before Christmas or Dr. Seuss, the shop can appear novelty driven at times.

ASTRO MIKE   **30**
5-25-2 JINGUMAE, SHIBUYA-KU
03-3499-2588, WWW.MIKE-TOYS.COM
HOURS: 12:00 — 20:00

Offering a heavy selection of American action figure toys, along with knickknacks and lots of classic science fiction novelties, Astro Mike is a wide net of inexpensive toy trinkets that could best be summarized as "new retro."

MISHKA 41
3-28-5, JINGUMAE, SHIBUYA-KU
03-6447-2813, WWW.MISHKANYC.COM
HOURS: 12:00 — 20:00

Just when you thought you had seen everything Tokyo had to offer, along came a couple kids from New York to add a little more off the wall aesthetic to your visual feast. The Tokyo Mishka store features everything that you would expect from these renegades–giant bear heads, squid eyeball chandeliers, horror and rock-n-roll reference galore, and even a few toys. With their own signature Bootleg kaiju, as well as collaborations with Secret Base and BountyxHunter, Mishka is a surprising mix of punk, purple and panic in every corner.

EROSTIKA 21
3-15-8 #208, JINGUMAE, SHIBUYA-KU
03-5775-0924, WWW.EROSTIKA.NET
HOURS: 12:00 — 20:00

Best known for his voluptuous, retro artwork for rock posters and album covers, and for maintaining an impeccable personal appearance with stylish suits and custom wrestling masks, Rockin' Jelly Bean has managed to simultaneously keep his identity a secret and boost his public image. At his custom shop, Erostika, you can find a wide variety of t-shirts, posters, buttons, and prints embellished with the artist's signature work. On special events, Rockin' Jelly Bean has collaborated with Japanese vinyl company Rumble Monsters to create multiple colorways of Pharaohs and Damnedron that are exclusive to this shop. With a fun, outgoing staff, Erostika is the kind of shop you will find only in Japan.

HARAJUKU

05
BLISTER
4-31-6, JINGUMAE, SHIBUYA-KU
03-5412-0911, WWW.BLISTER.JP
HOURS: 11:00 — 20:30

For anyone remotely interested in anything action figure or Star Wars oriented, Blister should be your first stop. Blister has anything and everything you knew existed, as well as a steady stream of toy collaborations and unique products available only at their store. Most well known for their Star Wars specialty and exclusive items, Blister is the biggest single source of new-release action figure items in Tokyo, and possibly even in Japan. Named after the traditional action figure packaging style (a heavyweight printed "card" with a plastic "blister" attached to hold the figure), Blister is an action figure lover's heaven.

HARAJUKU

HARAJUKU STREET FASHION

06, 07, 08, 09, 10, 11, 12, 15, 17, 19, 23, 24, 25, 26, 27

In Harajuku, a maze of twisty side alleys and meandering streets, the main draw is the myriad specialty shops of every size, shape, and brand conceivable. With competition for the latest in fashion always at a fever pitch, shops come and go with regularity, only to be replaced seemingly overnight. No stone has been left unturned in this neighborhood, so any decent or indecent location has been used to its maximum advantage. With this in mind, no map of the area can ever be truly current or accurate, but many of the major names stay put for extended periods of time before reinventing themselves, sometimes only blocks away. Kinetics (07), Neighborhood (10), Ice Cream (06), Madfoot (24), Real Mad Hectic (25), Invisible Man (27), Xlarge/X-girl (26), Supreme (23), Beams Tee (15), Undefeated (12), and Stüssy (11) are here, to name just a few, but there are plenty more for you to discover on your own.

59

29

KIDDY LAND
6-1-9 JINGUMAE, SHIBUYA-KU
03-3409-3431, WWW.KIDDYLAND.CO.JP
HOURS: 10:00 — 18:00, CLOSED THE THIRD TUESDAY OF EACH MONTH

Another of Tokyo's well-known toy stores, Kiddy Land is actually a new toy store with a heavy emphasis on cuteness. Most interesting for tourists seems to be the fact that the store is six stories tall, with something different on each floor. With Gundam, Godzilla, and boy toys located near the top, Kiddy Land is the perfect place to find gifts, from affordable to outrageous, for the kid or adult on your list. Kiddy Land is also a bit of a cultural landmark, even appearing in the *Megazone 23* anime.

AOYAMA

36
ORIGINAL FAKE
OH BLDG., B1F, 5-3-25 MINAMIAOYAMA, MINATO-KU
3-3499-3333, WWW.ORIGINAL-FAKE.COM
HOURS: 12:00 — 20:00

No detail was left untouched in this Aoyama shop, one of the most aesthetically stunning spaces in all of Tokyo. With a larger-than-life anatomical Companion standing guard at its entrance, Original Fake is the flagship store for the artist KAWS. With both sides of a bisected shop lined in glazed or unglazed custom ceramic tile, and nearly invisible glass cases, Original Fake is a boutique first and a toy store second. Since opening in 2006, Original Fake has become the first (and usually only) place to get the latest KAWS figures and clothes. With clothing and toy prices reflecting ultra-limited availability and impeccable attention to detail, lines form early in the morning (or even the night before) for every new release.

- HIGHLIGHT SHOPS
- SECONDARY SHOPS
- POINTS OF INTEREST
- LANDMARKS
- KOBAN POLICE
- YAMANOTE
- SŌBU LOCAL

SHINJUKU

Famous for its high-rises, hotels, shopping, and massive train station, Shinjuku has a few toy stores worth stopping into as well. Take the east exit for Kabukicho, which will put you in front of a small plaza, directly across from a large television screen. From here, cross the plaza, take a right, and head down one short block to the Kinokuniya building (01), which is next door to one of the two Citibank (08b) locations in Shinjuku.

From here you can walk either around the block or through the Kinokuniya building to get to Forest Comic and DVD (02), as well as Sakuraya Hobby (03). Sakuraya is always full of new and late-season toys, and its second floor has a large variety of new toys and candy toys.

Hidden down the side streets from here are the Stüssy store (04) and the designer toy store Few Many (05). At Japanese vinyl manufacturer Wonderwall's signature shop, the product mix is a surprising blend of their own products and select outside brands. Just around the corner is housewares shop Franc Franc (06) and the Shinjkuku Disc Union punk shop (07).

On the opposite side of the station is superstore Yodobashi (09), with a basement full of brand-new toys at discount prices. Both a Citibank (08a) and a post office are nearby in case you need to make a cash withdrawal.

01_ KINOKUNIYA **02_** FOREST COMIC + DVD **03_** SAKURAYA HOBBY **04_** STÜSSY **05_** FEW MANY **06_** FRANC FRANC **07_** DISC UNION **08A/08B_** CITIBANK ATM **09_** YODOBASHI

SAKURAYA HOBBY 03
3-17-17 SHINJUKU, SHINJUKU-KU
03-3226-6868, WWW.SAKURAYA.CO.JP/SHOP/SHI_HOBY.HTML
HOURS: 10:00 — 21:00

Another of the electronic/video game/toy crossover stores, Sakuraya has a good selection of toys on the second floor, emphasizing new toys or last season's toys at a deep discount. The selection varies and can never be predicted, but the shelves are always full.

YODOBASHI 09
1-11-1 NISHI-SHINJUKU, SHINJUKU-KU
03-3346-1010, WWW.YODOBASHI.COM
HOURS: 9:30 — 22:00

Well known for its varied selection of anything electronic, the Shinjuku Yodobashi store has a wide selection of toys hidden in its basement. From model kits and Kamen Rider to video games and infant toys, everything is usually priced 10 to 20 percent below retail. This is a hot spot for super robot, sentai, and chogokin collectors.

FEW MANY 05
3-17-21 SHINJUKU, SHINJUKU-KU
03-3353-2532, WWW.FEWMANY.COM
HOURS: 12:00 — 20:00

Hiding in an unassuming side alley is designer toy store Few Many. In this home shop for Wonderwall, collaboration toys, tees, and other gifts share shelf space with a curated stock of outside brands. Rare shop-only releases and an eclectic selection make every trip to Few Many different from the last.

- HIGHLIGHT SHOPS
- SECONDARY SHOPS
- POINTS OF INTEREST
- LANDMARKS
- KOBAN POLICE

YAMANOTE
SŌBU LOCAL

NAKANO

If the Tokyo toy community had a nerve center, Nakano would be it. Home to the highest density of toy shops in the entire city, this little residential neighborhood is much more than meets the eye.

Take the north exit from the train station, and across the plaza, you should see the scalloped entrance to the Sun Mall, an open-air mall with a covered ceiling. Walk the length of the mall, past the shoe, t-shirt, and pantyhose dealers and McDonald's. Go all the way to the end of the mall; even when you second-guess yourself and think you have gone too far, just keep going. You may not even notice when you exit the Sun Mall and enter the Broadway Mall, but when you do, there will be an escalator and a set of stairs to your right. The escalator goes to the third floor, while the stairs go to all floors. We suggest taking the stairs. Sixty-four toy stores are spread across the second, third, and fourth floors, and visiting them all will take hours.

For those of you who do notice the Broadway Mall demarcation, take a quick left, and about thirty feet down is a set of stairs on the right leading up to one of Nakano's best shops, Moda-Yu (01).

Besides the plentiful Mandarake shops, the Broadway Mall is filled with shops, both great and not so great, covering every conceivable aspect of toy collecting. Our favorites include the Robot Robot case shops on the third floor (46 and 47), Bow Wow case shop (15), Toy Shop Rough (11 and 12), the Antique Toy Shop (24), and the One Up (31, 32, and 64) shops located on floors three and four. Any store can have amazing stock on any given day, so we generally spend about four hours checking them all out.

01_ MODA-YU-Q-TE 02-64_ NAKANO BROADWAY TOY SHOPS

SECOND FLOOR

02-64

NAKANO BROADWAY MALL

01

TWIN PLAZA

BIKE GARAGE

SUN MALL ENTRANCE

KFC

NORTH EXIT

NAKANO STATION

01
MODA-YU-Q-TE
SEE MAP ON PAGES 66–67
03-5380-3512

The only shop in Nakano not actually located inside the Broadway Mall, Moda-Yu is also one of the neighborhood's finest. Moda-Yu is located about thirty feet to the left of the main mall entrance, and up one narrow flight of stairs. Inside you will find a deep stock of a wide variety of toys, from vintage vinyl and die-cast to new capsule figures. The store is jam-packed to the ceiling and the walls are bulging with toys, so leave your backpack and bags by the door to avoid inadvertently knocking something over. Moda-Yu's pleasant staff and reasonable prices ensure that everyone can enjoy a stop here.

線路に物を落された方は
駅係員にお申し出ください

01, 08, 14, 19, 20, 22, 23, 25–27, 29, 33–38, 54, 57–60, 62

MANDARAKE
5-52-15 NAKANO, NAKANO-KU
03-3228-0007, WWW.MANDARAKE.CO.JP/ENGLISH/SHOP/NKN.HTML
HOURS: 12:00 — 20:00

Distributed liberally over three floors and twenty-three locations in the Broadway Mall, Mandarake has one of almost everything. With shops devoted to mini-erasers, manga, R/C cars, and cosplay, Mandarake covers the spectrum like no one else can. Mandarake's most prominent shop, New Special, is nothing that the name implies. Guarded by a larger-than-life Tetsujin-28, the shop is home to all vintage toys, jumbos, die-cast, or vinyls that have not been pulled for their semiannual auction. Other prominent Mandarake stores include Special 3, on the third floor, which specializes in secondhand current toys, and a tin and advertising-display shop on the fourth floor. Describing Mandarake's complete inventory is impossible, but you can discover that for yourself as you walk the halls of the Broadway Mall.

NAKANO

SECOND FLOOR
01_ MANDARAKE NEW SPECIAL (VINTAGE STORE)
02_ CASE SHOP
03_ HIGH-GRADE SHOP
04/05/06_ CASE SHOPS
07_ BOX KEY CASE SHOP
08_ MANDARAKE AMAZING (AMERICAN TOYS)
09/10_ CUBE STYLE CASE SHOPS
11/12_ TOY SHOPS ROUGH CASE SHOPS
13_ CASE SHOP
14_ MANDARAKE DRAWING
15_ BOW WOW CASE SHOP
16_ CAR SHOP
17_ GAMES WORKSHOP
18_ CASE SHOP
19_ MANDARAKE GACHA TEN
20_ MANDARAKE CARS
21_ A. BARTH (MISC. TOYS)
22_ MANDARAKE LIVE
23_ MANDARAKE GALAXY
24_ ANTIQUE TOYS
25_ MANDARAKE UFO 2
26_ MANDARAKE GIRLS' SHOP
27_ MANDARAKE UFO CASE
28_ CASE SHOP
29_ MANDARAKE UFO CASE
    (NOW FILLED WITH VINYL)

2F
(ENTRANCE)

THIRD FLOOR
30_ ROBOT ROBOT
31_ ONE UP CASES
32_ ONE UP MAIN SHOP
33_ MANDARAKE BUYING STATION
34_ MANDARAKE RPG
35_ MANDARAKE SPECIAL 3
(NEW + USED CURRENT TOYS)
36_ MANDARAKE MANGA
37_ MANDARAKE MANGA
38_ MANDARAKE CASES
39_ HAIKURO TOY (HIGH-GRADE FIGURES)
40_ HIGH-GRADE SHOP
41_ CASE SHOP
42_ BLOX AMERICAN TOYS
43_ AMOJU CASE SHOP
44_ K'S WAVE CASE SHOP
45_ ROBOT ROBOT (NEW + AMERICAN TOYS)
46_ ROBOT ROBOT CASE SHOP
47_ ROBOT ROBOT CASE SHOP
48_ GACHAPON MACHINES
49_ CAR SHOP
50_ COSPLAY SHOP
51_ GACHAPON MACHINES
52_ NEW TOY SHOP
53_ CASE SHOP

3F
(ENTRANCE)

4F
(ENTRANCE)

FOURTH FLOOR
54_ MANDARAKE (ADVERTISING AND TIN)
55_ WEST CASE DOLL SHOP
56_ CASE SHOP
57_ MANDARAKE MICRO CASES (MINI-ERASERS)
58_ MANDARAKE CELLS
59_ MANDARAKE MICRO (MINI-ERASERS)
60_ MANDARAKE COSPLAY
61_ CASE SHOP
62_ MANDARAKE MANGA
63_ GACHAPON MACHINES
64_ ONE UP CASES AND CAPSULE SHOP

	HIGHLIGHT SHOPS
	SECONDARY SHOPS
	POINTS OF INTEREST
	LANDMARKS
	KOBAN POLICE
	YAMANOTE
	SŌBU LOCAL

KOENJI

Just a single short stop on the Sobu line from Nakano is the neighborhood of Koenji. A local area with a vibrant mix of used-record, vintage clothing, and toy stores, Koenji is Nakano's punk rock or heavy-metal older brother. Rarely traversed by the average tourist, Koenji feels like a modern neighborhood, with few traditional buildings but simple, functional architecture. Slower-paced than some of the larger neighborhoods, Koenji is home to vintage-toy shops Gojira-Ya and Ichiban-Boshi, as well as Gargamel's Thrash Out flagship store and Boy Records, one of Tokyo's oldest punk record stores.

01_ YANCHOME CAFÉ (2F) **02_** BONE BAG (2F)/RECORD SHOP BASE (3F) **03_** THRASH OUT/GARGAMEL (2F)
04_ WELL ROUNDED **05_** ICHIBAN-BOSHI **06_** MAMEGYORAI **07_** BOY RECORDS **08_** GODZILLA-YA

KOENJI STATION

- 08
- 07
- PAL SIGN
- FOUNTAIN
- GRILL CORNER
- 01
- 06
- FRESHNESS
- 02
- SHOPPING DISTRICT
- LAWSON'S
- 05
- 03
- SUNKUS
- 04

When you arrive in Koenji, there is only one exit from the station, but immediately after exiting, you will need to take a right and go to the south side of the station. When you emerge from the station, to your right you should see a small fountain and an abstract metal structure. Along the main street, you will pass Bone Bag (02, 2F) and Record Shop Base (02, 3F), which have a good selection of new and used records.

Another two and a half quick blocks down is Thrash Out (03), vinyl toy manufacturer Gargamel's flagship store. Just look for the small light-up sign and the gachapon machine full of giant toys, and then head up the stairs to Gargamel's wood-trimmed hideout. After picking up the latest shop exclusives, you can continue down the same road to Well Rounded (04), which is a Hot Wheels shop, or cross the street to Ichiban-Boshi (05), which offers plenty to buy and even more to see. From there, it's a quick jaunt up the back streets or main streets to the train tracks. Following the tracks west, you will pass Boy Records (07) on the left. Look out for the small white sandwich board out front, because it's easy to miss. In a dark wood building with a narrow staircase leading up to the second floor, Boy is one of Tokyo's oldest punk record stores, specializing in crust, hardcore, and political punk but including a nice sampling of other subgenres, as well as plenty of rare, out-of-print records. Be warned: Boy only accepts cash payments, so credit cards won't work here.

Just past Boy Records is Godzilla-Ya (08). One of Tokyo's older shops, Godzilla-Ya is just up yet another narrow set of stairs, and on the left-hand side. Filled wall to wall with vinyl, die-cast, jumbos, and more, Godzilla-Ya can at times feel more like a garage sale than a toy shop. You never know what you can find here.

Heading back to the station, feel free to wander the side streets and PAL Shopping Arcade for other miscellaneous shops, including Mamegyorai (06). If you need a snack, the second-floor Yanchome Café (01) offers a wide variety of food.

MR. CONTACT: POSSESSING TWICE THE PERSONALITY OF ANY OTHER OVER-THE-COUNTER DRUG, MR. CONTACT IS A LIVING PILL READY TO BATTLE THE ILLS OF THE WORLD. IF ONLY OUR COLD REMEDIES WERE THIS EXCITING.

03
THRASH OUT/GARGAMEL
2-51-9 2F KOENJI, SUGINAMI-KU
03-3315-6570, WWW.GARGAMEL.JP/THRASHOUT
HOURS: NO SET HOURS; VARY ON WEEKDAYS OR ON PRODUCT-RELEASE DAYS

A hefty combination of heavy metal and dark wood will entice you at the top of the stairs at Thrash Out. Thrash out is home to and the signature store of one of Japan's finest new toy companies, Gargamel. The founders, longtime friends Kiyoka, Ikeda, and Chanmen, pay homage to Japan's lesser-known kaiju and recreate them in new ways, much to the delight of their fans. The store has a visual history of Gargamel's figural friends, as well as a few key vintage and newer vinyl toys. Thanks to exclusive collaborations with Tim Biskup, Bwana Spoons, Le Merde, Martin Ontiveros, and Super7, stock often goes fast, so don't wait if you hear of a new release. The shop is usually open just on release days. but feel free to knock anytime to see if anyone is there to let you shop.

05
ICHIBAN-BOSHI
3-37-19 MINAMI, SUGINAMI KOENJI
03-3313-8025, WWW.1BAN-BOSHI.COM
HOURS: 14:00 — 20:00

A great vintage store just off the beaten path, Ichiban-Boshi has a huge selection of toys for almost all collectors. Cases of rare vintage vinyls mix freely with new figures and reproductions, while quality die-cast and Jumbo Machinders make a stand in the side cases. Formerly located in Shinjuku, Ichiban-Boshi relocated to Koenji in late 2005 and has helped make the area a collectors' destination. Prices are generally reasonable across the board, but some of the rare pieces are priced accordingly. Another interesting component of Ichiban-Boshi is their custom figure of Ryusei Ninja, developed as a collaboration with RealxHead. In addition to a friendly staff, store-only releases of their figure offer extra incentive to pay this shop a visit.

GODZILLA-YA   08
3-67-1 KOENJI, SUGINAMI-KU
03-3336-3178, WWW.PLALA.OR.JP/GODZILLAYA
HOURS: 14:00 — 21:00, CLOSED WEDNESDAY

A rare holdover from the heyday of Japanese toy collecting, Godzilla-Ya is a true institution. While it is packed to the gills with nearly every kind of toy imaginable, Godzilla-Ya is a hit-or-miss kind of store. Upon first impression it can appear a bit junky, but there is a method to Godzilla-Ya's madness, and if you look in just the right place, you may strike toy gold. Prices fluctuate wildly and seem to be a little more beat down than usual, but so does the merchandise, so condition-sensitive completists, be warned. Regardless, shops like this paved the way for many others, so stop and show your respect.

MAMEGYORAI   06
3-56-1 KOENJI, MINAMI

A self-proclaimed action figure and comics store, Mamegyorai is mostly just action figures, with a bent toward American toys, although it has the occasional shop exclusive with smaller Japanese manufacturers. A wide variety of new and deadstock figures from the recent past fills the shelves, as well as a heaping handful of Living Dead dolls for those who are interested.

WELL ROUNDED   04
2-24-23 MINAMI, SUGINAMI KOENJI
03-3317-2242

A Hot Wheels and car collectors' destination, Well Rounded is a fun shop at the south end of Koenji. Very serious about their miniature machines, the staff are always ready to talk cars. If you collect any of the above, make sure to stop by.

- HIGHLIGHT SHOPS
- SECONDARY SHOPS
- POINTS OF INTEREST
- LANDMARKS
- KOBAN POLICE

YAMANOTE

SŌBU LOCAL

KICHIJOJI

Kichijoji is a large neighborhood on the west side of Tokyo that is home to a surprising number of Western expatriates. The immediate area outside the north exit of the train station is a fairly typical concentration of large and small shops, with two international ATMs nearby, at either the post office or Citibank. Just behind the area's main façade is a large gachapon parlor called At First (01), designer t-shirt shop Graniph (02), and a wide range of books at Books Ruhe (03). Around the corner, you will see the gigantic and always humorous DOG WIZ sign, which leads you to the main road through this section of Kichijoji. Just before you reach the T-shaped intersection, in the basement to your right is Tonkatsu (04), a restaurant shrouded in mystery, highly guarded from the public by generations of shadowy, international toy purists. Could we be more vague?

If you turn right at the T-shaped intersection, Wave Be-J (06) is located three blocks down the road on the left-hand side. Full of new toys, from gachapon to chogokin to action figures, they carry a tantalizing sampling of everything. From there, go back one street, over one block, and down the side street. Before you hit Hotel Aland is Toy Cats Showcase (05), hidden in the basement of the building. Toy Cats Showcase specializes in new and old Star Wars items, and features an interesting assortment of newer used items and vintage toys in the showcases.

When you return to the train station, check out the department store Yuzawa (07), located on the south side, which has a good selection of new toys on the eighth floor.

01_ AT FIRST 02_ GRANIPH 03_ BOOKS RUHE 04_ TONKATSU 05_ TOY CATS SHOWCASE 06_ WAVE BE-J 07_ YUZAWA

KICHIJOJI

RIGHT:
WHEN YOU LEAVE THE NORTH EXIT AT KICHIJOJI, THIS WILL BE YOUR VIEW. FROM HERE, IT IS A SHORT WALK TO ANY OF THE SHOPS IN KICHIJOJI.

TOY CATS SHOWCASE   05
1-26-4 HORIUCHI BLDG. B1, KICHIJOJI HOMMACHI, MUSASHINO-KU
04-2223-1055, WWW.TOYCATS.NET/INDEX.HTML
HOURS: 12:00 — 20:00

In a less obvious location that is well worth the hunt, Toy Cats Showcase has a large selection of Star Wars toys, consignment toys, and a few nice vintage pieces. With a friendly staff and friendly prices, Toy Cats Showcase is always a fun shop to visit.

WAVE BE-J   06
1-11-20 KICHIJOJI EAST, MUSASHINO-KU
04-2221-0733, WWW.BE-J.COM
HOURS: WEEKDAYS 12:00 — 23:00, WEEKENDS 11:00 — 23:00

A comprehensive toy and hobby store, Wave Be-J has all the latest Gundam and chogokin action figures, gachapon, and model kits. There are no vintage toys, and prices range from standard retail to slightly expensive, but not offensive.

- 🟢 **HIGHLIGHT SHOPS**
- 🟢 **SECONDARY SHOPS**
- 🟡 **POINTS OF INTEREST**
- ⬜ **LANDMARKS**
- **KOBAN POLICE**
- **YAMANOTE**
- **SŌBU LOCAL**

AKIHABARA

"Bright Lights, Big City of Dreams"—this might as well be the theme song of Akihabara, which boasts more neon and signage than most other places in Tokyo, but the area is usually referred to simply as Electric Town. Just beneath its glowing veneer, Akihabara is also home to the *otaku*. The term may conjure up annoying mental images of older, single, overweight men with glasses who play video games and watch animation all night, but in Akihabara you can find the alpha of this stereotype, as well as a million evolutionary offshoots.

For most anime, robot, or sentai series fans, Akihabara is your primary destination. The streets are littered with toy shops, ranging from new to old, small to large, and carrying just about anything you can imagine, as well as a few things you shouldn't. Along the way, just about any electronic gadget you never knew you needed is also available, so stock up on digital cameras, video games, and cell phones that are far too advanced to be compatible with Western technology.

01_ YODOBASHI-AKIBA **02_** GAMERS **03_** RADIO KAIKAN **04_** ASOBIT CITY HOBBY **05_** ASOBIT CITY CHARA **06_** YANIGAWA SOFT **07_** MANDARAKE **08_** CREPE STAND **09_** ROBOT-HEROKAN **10_** COLLECTABLES TOKYO **11_** LIBERTY 7 **12_** HOBBY FIGURE **13_** LIBERTY 9 **14_** TOYS GOLDEN AGE **15_** CHIOCCIO@PIZZERIA

05
06
07
08
09
10
11
12
13
14
15
01

CHUO DORI STREET

TOKYO METRO
SUBWAY
GINZA LINE
G-14
SUE HIROCHO
STATION

KURAMEBASHI-DORI

ATM

01

YODOBASHI–AKIBA

1-1 SOTOKANDA, CHIYODA-KU
03-5209-1010, WWW.YODOBASHI-AKIBA.COM
HOURS: 9:30 — 22:00

Yodobashi is an electronics superstore with floors devoted to almost every object that can be operated with a power or USB cord. Interestingly enough, the sixth floor is home to a wide variety of video games, but an even wider variety of toys. Like all great superstores, they carry it all—from toddler toys and Apanman squeakies to the latest in sentai superheroes and scale-model kits. In addition to their broad selection, Yodobashi's other great allure is their prices, which are usually 20 percent below conventional retail. It's not unusual to see a first-time visitor going wild on Yodobashi prices and filling bags' worth of toy gold for the trip home. Additionally, Yodobashi has the largest gachapon aisle you will find in Akihabara (or anywhere else, for that matter) for all the mini-size collectors looking for the latest releases. As Yodobashi is open later than most collector shops, we recommend saving it for last, unless you want to carry your haul for the rest of the day.

AKIHABARA

Welcome to Akihabara, home to the second-largest group of toy shops in Tokyo (behind Nakano) and the largest group of otaku in all their various and uncomfortable forms. As you get off the Sobu or Yamanote train, head for the Electric Town exit. Upon exiting the turnstiles, take a left, which should put you on a side street facing just to the left of Radio Kaikan (03) and Asobit City Hobby (04). Though they occupy separate buildings, the overlapping signage makes the distinction between buildings slightly less obvious. Both buildings are full of various case shops, small consignment shops, and a general toy store carrying Star Wars and character goods. On the same side of the street as the train tracks is Gamers (02), a general store of all things otaku. Just past this is the main street of Akihabara, Chuo-Dori. (Just look for the LAOX sign if you get turned around.)

Take your time as you travel down Chuo-Dori, stopping in a wide array of toy stores. We suggest walking down one side of the street and coming back on the other. As happens in Nakano, you can experience toy burnout in Akihabara, so pace yourself or come back for more later.

The north side of the street is home to the area's smaller shops, while larger shops are typically on the south side. Asobit City Chara (05) is across the street and has six floors full of character goods, but the volume of quality stores nearby prevents it from being a highly trafficked destination. Yanigawa Soft (06) is an electronics store with a plentiful supply of chogokin androbot series toys on the second floor.

Two short blocks off of Chuo Dori is the newest and largest of the Mandarake stores, Mandarake Akihabara (07). This seven-story flagship store is packed to the gills with everything imaginable, from affordable to insane, and has some of the most impressive toys and prices in all of Tokyo. Then again, sometimes the hardest part is finding what you are looking for, not paying for it. Just down the side alleys from Mandarake is Robot-Herokan (09), a small but nicely maintained vintage store specializing in chogokin, and Collectables Tokyo (10), a new shop full of Kubricks and gachapon toys.

Cross the street at the intersection of Chuo-Dori and Kuramaebashi-Dori, and you'll begin to enter the big toy stores that anchor Akihabara's reputation. First up is the overstuffed Toys Golden Age (14), which is one step away from being a crime scene and is literally bursting at the seams with toys. Right next door is Liberty 9 (13), an eight-floor toy store with something for everyone. The polar opposite of Toys Golden Age, Liberty 9 arranges its displays so carefully as to sometimes create too much space. Next up is Hobby Figure (12), just off Chuo-Dori to the south. Part of the same Liberty family as Liberty 9, it is another multi-story shop with a very similar layout, and even more stock. To make it even more complicated, Liberty 7 (11) is the third of these megastores. You can burn out easily if you visit all three of the Liberty shops in a row.

On your way back to the train station, there is a great crêpe stand (08) to the left, or, if you're in the mood for more than a snack, try Chioccio@Pizzeria (15) at the base of the building one block back. There is also an ATM in this building, around the corner.

Now that you have seen everything else in Akihabara, it's time to hit Yodobashi-Akiba (01). Lots of people make this their first stop in Akihabara, but unless you want to carry these bags the whole time, we recommend saving it for last (its late closing time makes this easy to do). Yodobashi is a giant department store, and the sixth floor is stocked to the brim with toys and video games. Everything is brand new and priced 10 to 20 percent below retail. All fans of chogokin, model kits, Transformers, video games, or anything new toy-wise owe it to themselves to stop in, as no one leaves empty handed.

SATO-CHAN:
THE CUTEST ORANGE ELEPHANT ON THE PLANET, SATO-CHAN IS ALL OVER TOKYO. A MASCOT FOR A POPULAR CHAIN OF DRUGSTORES, SATO-CHAN IS OFTEN ACCOMPANIED BY HIS LITTLE SISTER, A PINK ELEPHANT NAMED SATO KO-CHAN.

AKIHABARA

11, 12, 13

LIBERTY 7, HOBBY FIGURE, LIBERTY 9
WWW.LIBERTY-SHOP.CO.JP/ANNAI/AKIBACHIZU.HTML
WWW.LIBERTY-SHOP.CO.JP
HOURS: 11:00 — 20:00

These three stores, all part of the Liberty group of stores and the anchors of the Akihabara toy scene, are almost identical in setup and point of view. All are multi-story shops with floors dedicated to particular genres of collecting. The bottom floors are generally all chogokin and super robot related, with other floors dedicated to gachapon figures, anime, military, RPG, action figures, Disney, and other character goods. Vinyl pieces of any sort are few and far between, and all stock is secondhand, yet the latest releases are always here. Prices are usually quite good on anything considered out of date or only marginally popular, while the hot new releases make up for any savings you may find on the older items.

07

MANDARAKE AKIHABARA
3-11-2 6F SOTOKANDA, CHIYODA-KU
03-3252-7007, WWW.MANDARAKE.CO.JP/ENGLISH/SHOP/AKB.HTML
HOURS: 11:00 — 20:30

The newest of the Mandarake stores, the Akihabara version is also the most grand. Housed in a brand-new black building Mandarake built for itself, the Mandarake Akihabara is now the largest (and most expensive) of the Mandarake stores. With its large scale, this Mandarake has plenty for everyone, and lines to get in even start forming about 15 minutes prior to opening time. Eight floors of toys, manga, die-cast, and Gachapon fill every corner of this mega-Mandarake making it a must-stop for every kind of collector.

AKIHABARA

ASOBIT CITY HOBBY   04
1-15-18 SOTOKANDA, CHIYODA-KU
03-5298-3581, WWW.AKIBAASOBIT.JP
HOURS: 10:00 — 22:00

ASOBIT CITY CHARA   05
1-13-2 SOTOKANDA, CHIYODA-KU
03-3251-3100, WWW.AKIBAASOBIT.JP
HOURS: 10:00 — 22:00

Six and seven floors, respectively, the Asobit stores are multilevel monsters stocked with every kind of new toy, video game, character good, or hobby item you could want. However, their average retail pricing and apparent lack of enthusiasm mean that you will probably end up shopping elsewhere, and have a better time doing it.

ROBOT-HEROKAN   09
3-10-6 MARUWA BLDG.B1F SOTOKANDA, CHIYODA-KU
0120-135-163
HOURS: 11:00 — 20:00

A small shop selling used toys, Robot Herokan focuses on Transformers, Gundam, Tokusatsu, and sentai, with a few vinyl toys thrown in for good measure. The prices are good and the shop owner is friendly, but more than three people can turn this tiny space into a claustrophobic's worst nightmare.

COLLECTABLES TOKYO   10
3-9-8 SOTOKANDA CHIYODA-KU
03-5294-6171, WWW.COLLECTABLES.JP
HOURS: 11:00 — 20:00, SUNDAYS & HOLIDAYS 11:00 — 19:00

Following all the newest trends in micro-collecting, Collectables Tokyo is full of all the latest candy toys, Kubricks, Be@bricks, and anything else you can think of that is three inches tall or smaller. Unless you are a candy-toy completist, you can skip this store.

14

TOYS GOLDEN AGE
4-7-2 KOBAYASHI, CHIYODA-KU
03-5256-0012, WWW.GEOCITIES.JP/CYCLONE_0999/ANNAI.JPG
HOURS: 11:30 — 21:00

The last shop on the main Akihabara drag, Toys Golden Age is also one of the best. While many of the other shops have divided their stock on numerous floors, Toys Golden Age has stuffed it all into a single level. Toys are stacked literally two or three deep in front of showcases and behind the counter, so picking out individual items can be a test of your visual stamina. Take your time, drop your bags at the door, and get to searching—rarities, common items, and obscurities from just about every genre are hidden here, but you may have to work a bit for them. The staff are happy to move and rearrange things to get to hidden gems, but they do not speak any English, so employ your best version of toy sign language for your archeological adventure.

AKIHABARA

YANIGAWA SOFT 06
SEE MAP ON PAGES 84–85 FOR DIRECTIONS

Yanigawa Soft is one of the typical video game/electronics and toy retailers that you can find all over Akihabara, as well as Tokyo at large. The second floor of Yanigawa Soft has a good selection of robot and chogokin toys.

RADIO KAIKAN 03
1-15-16 SOTOKANDA, CHIYODA-KU
03-3251-3711, WWW.RADIOKAIKAN.ORG
HOURS: 10:00 — 21:00

Filled with toys, anime, and manga shops, Radio Kaikan can be a thrilling and scary place. K-Books, on the third floor, is a famous manga bookstore, and floors four, five, and six are home to a wide variety of shops. But be warned — this is the first of many buildings with a variety of dubious adult content, hentai, and eyebrow-lifting items right next to traditional toy sellers.

GAMERS 02
1-14-7 SOTOKANDA, CHIYODA-KU
03-5298-8720, WWW.BROCCOLI.CO.JP/GAMERS
HOURS: 11:00 — 21:00

You either love or hate Gamers, a one-stop haven for all things otaku. You either love or hate Gamers. Each floor is tailored to a different kind of fanaticism; toys and models are on the seventh floor.

	HIGHLIGHT SHOPS
	SECONDARY SHOPS
	POINTS OF INTEREST
	LANDMARKS
	KOBAN POLICE

YAMANOTE

SŌBU LOCAL

KOIWA/KAMEIDO

Koiwa is a small neighborhood closer to the outskirts of Tokyo. A forty-five-minute train ride from Shibuya on the Sobu local, Koiwa is very residential and free of tourists, other than those few daring souls coming to shop for toys.

Down to only two stores now (a third has since moved to Nakano), Koiwa is home to one of the most famous shops in all of Tokyo—Third Uncle/Characters (02). All that remains of the original Third Uncle family of shops, Characters is densely packed, full of more rare toys than any other shop in Tokyo, and more expensive than all the other shops combined.

When you arrive at the Koiwa station, take the main exit, then turn right as you pass the turnstiles. This should put you in front of department store Ito-Yokado, which has a few new toys on the sixth floor and a few candy toys in the basement.

Taking the road on the left side of Ito-Yokado will get you to the main road of Kuramaebashi-Dori. On a side note, you will pass Three Cousin (01), which is artist Pushead's favorite *negima* in the area.

After you are through with Characters, go back to Kuramaebashi-Dori, head west for four blocks, and take a left turn down a neighborhood side street by a small power station to visit Manga Beya (03), originally one of the only remaining tin toy and advertising premium shops. Its owner began producing vinyl toys under the name Shikaruna in 2008, and has become very popular with a new generation of collectors.

01_ THREE COUSIN 02_ THIRD UNCLE/CHARACTERS 03_ MANGA BEYA/SHIKARUNA

02

KURAMAEBASHI-DORI STREET

01

MR. DONUT

ITO-YOKADO

KOIWA STATION
EXIT

02

THIRD UNCLE/CHARACTERS
3-34-8 NISHI-KOIWA, EDOGAWA-KU
03-3659-5545, WWW.THIRD-UNCLE.COM
HOURS: 13:00 — 21:00, CLOSED MONDAY

One of Tokyo's best-known shops, Characters houses the crème de la crème of toy stock for every collector, with a selection so rare as to stop even the most jaded aficionados in their tracks. One of the original trifecta of dominant toy shops (like Forest Gangu and the original Third Uncle), Characters carries on their original legacy to this day. Beyond its impressive selection, Characters' other legacy may well be its prices. Never afraid to aim for the sky, Characters may have all the toys your heart desires, but your wallet may not be able to handle it. A must-see for any first-time or serious toy collector.

KAMEIDO

For those of you interested in shopping for new toys, there is a Toys-R-Us located close by, in the neighborhood of Kameido. Located four stops past Akihabara and three stops before you get to Koiwa, Kameido is an easy destiation for anyone headed to Koiwa. The Toys-R-Us is actually one of the best in the city, as it's rarely visited by tourists and is usually well stocked. To get there, exit the Sobu line at Kameido (which is on the north side of the tracks), and walk around the station to the south side. You will see the shopping center with Toys-R-Us just down the road running parallel to the train tracks. The Toys-R-Us is at the back of the mall area, along with (like at most malls) several somewhat questionable food choices. While there is surely something else worth mentioning about Kameido, we are not familiar with it, so let us know if you find anything.

MANGA BEYA/SHIKARUNA   03
SEE MAP ON PAGES 94–95 FOR DIRECTIONS

Originally known as a tin toy and vintage advertising and display store, Manga Beya is what you imagine toy stores must have looked like in years past. Today, after the recent launch of its own brand of vinyl figures under the company name Shikaruna, Manga Beya is seeing a resurgence in popularity. Chances are good that if you stop by on any given day, you may see the next wave of Shikaruna figures actually being planned or painted, all while you stare at cases full of upcoming sculpts, prototypes, and samples.

- HIGHLIGHT SHOPS
- SECONDARY SHOPS
- POINTS OF INTEREST
- LANDMARKS
- KOBAN POLICE
- YAMANOTE
- TOKYO TOYOKO LINE

EBISU/ DAIKANYAMA

Ebisu and Daikanyama are two adjacent neighborhoods that butt up against Shibuya's south side. Ebisu has two stores, Mr. Craft and Monster Japan, both of which specialize in American and Star Wars toys; Mr. Craft sells new toys, and Monster Japan sells vintage toys.

As you walk into Daikanyama, you will find the neighborhood a bit more sprawling and expansive than many Tokyo neighborhoods. Essentially, shops have opened up along the outside edge of the neighborhood, near the train tracks along Hachiman-Dori, or further down, in the quickly morphing area of "Daikanyama address." This general area holds the two main crossover toy shops, Junie Moon, the CWC flagship store and home to Blythe, and Stitch, a furniture, art, toy and home-accessories gallery. Stretching further, to fashion brands Devilock and Let It Ride, we are technically in the neighborhood of Naka-Meguro, but it is an equal walk from either station, so we have added it here for those who may be interested.

01_ MR. CRAFT 02_ MONSTER JAPAN 03_ SUPREME 04_ SILAS 05_ JUNIE MOON 06_ FRAMES CAFÉ 07_ STENDIG DESIGN 08_ ZAC PAC 09_ CACTUS 10_ STITCH 11_ MANGART 12_ HOLLYWOOD RANCH 13_ DEVILOCK 14_ LET IT RIDE 15_ GRANIPH (2ND FL.)

Upon arriving at Ebisu, take the west exit, which will put you in a large courtyard. Directly across the street, you should see a large Nova sign, which has an interesting metal sculpture of the god Ebisu on the left side, above the first floor.

Immediately around the corner on the right-hand side is Mr. Craft (01). In this six-story building of shops, the main store on the bottom floor is full of new character toys, especially Star Wars figures. The remaining floors are mostly full of mini R/C cars, with some consignment cases on the fifth floor. Just one quick block up is Monster Japan (02), another toy store devoted to Western character toys. Specializing more in monsters and Star Wars, they have a diverse array of new and old figures and a surprisingly high quantity of prototypes and test shots from *Star Wars*. At the large intersection two blocks ahead, you'll see a pork restaurant on the left called Butagoya. Having never eaten there, we can't recommend the food, but they do have an amazing mural that wraps around the top of the building.

To see more of the neighborhood, it is easiest to follow the tracks. Pass under an elevated railway and proceed one more block to an overpass road. The route along the way used to be covered in amazing graffiti by artists from all over the world, but most has been painted over, although KAMI and SASU recently painted the underside of the train bridge.

When you arrive at the elevated roadway, take the steps to your left, and you should be directly in front of hipster skate shop Supreme (03). A block and a half down from that is the English brand Silas (04). Across the street and another block down is big-eyed-doll heaven in the form of the shop Junie Moon (05), the CWC shop, which is home to the original big-eyed doll, Blythe. There are lots of little shops down the surrounding narrow streets, Frames Café (06) is good for a quick bite, and Stendig Design (07) is a neat little modern furniture store.

As you walk down Hachiman-Dori toward Daikainyama address, you will come upon a mix of older shops and very new, more upscale shops. On your left with be Zac-Pac (08), which carries toys of just about every make and description, and on your right, on the second floor, will be Cactus (09), which is a great kids' toy store. Just ahead on the right will be design shop Stitch (10). Stitch specializes in all facets of design and art, including toy design, and houses an art gallery, which often has shows with the latest up-and-coming artists. Just past Stitch and off to the right, the more upscale shopping begins, with many new stores arriving as we speak. Of note is the Beams T Mangart shop (11) and Hollywood Ranch (12), a fashion stop for over thirty years.

For those up for a little bit more walking, you can head over toward Naka-Meguro, where all sorts of shops line the alleys and side streets. Of note are punk fashion brand Devilock (13) and the outlaw-motorcycle-inspired Let It Ride (14), whose signage and display were all made by Japanese artist NUTS. As always, there is a Graniph close by as well, to make your lap around the area complete. As you head back, you can either return to Ebisu station or wander you way up to Shibuya station through the upper reaches of Daikan-yama, as it is a short walk.

THIS LITTLE PIGGY:
THE LARGE WRAPAROUND MURAL ABOVE BUTAGOYA IS A FUN AND HUMOROUS COLLECTION OF SCENES THAT SPANS THE ENTIRE FRONT OF THE BUILDING. PAINTED BY YUZZA IN 2006, IT IS A RECENT ADDITION TO THE EBISU WALKING TOUR.

EBISU/DAIKANYAMA

MONSTER JAPAN 02
1-6-1 3F EBISU WEST, SHIBUYA-KU
03-3463-3555, WWW.MONSTER-JAPAN.CO.JP
HOURS: 13:00 — 20:30

For the Star Wars or American-movie-monster enthusiast, Monster Japan is a great shop surrounded by new and vintage Western action figure–style toys, and vintage Universal Monsters, *Aliens*, and American sci-fi items. You'll be surprised that you can't find similar stores stateside. Monster Japan's sizable stash of Hasbro prototypes means you can obtain unique items here that you won't find in other shops.

JUNIE MOON 05
4-3 1F SARUGAKU-CHO, SHIBUYA-KU
WWW.JUNIEMOON.JP/INDEX.E.CGI
HOURS: TUE.–SAT. 12 — 20:00, SUN. 12 — 18:00; CLOSED MON.

Who knew that a big-eyed doll with changing eye color could become so popular? Nearly forty years after her introduction, Blythe has a loyal and fanatical following of collectors and customizers like few other dolls. Official Blythe licenser CWC shows off the latest in Blythe style and fashion at their Junie Moon shop, so that everyone can get a chance to buy these sought-after dolls.

MR. CRAFT 01
1-7-4 EBISU WEST
03-3461-2665, WWW.MRCRAFT.COM
HOURS: WEEKDAYS 12:00 — 22:00, WEEKENDS 11:00 — 22:00

At Mr. Craft, a six-story toy store, the bottom floor is chock full of action figures and a wide range of Star Wars items.
There are showcases on the fifth floor, and the rest of the floors are devoted to R/C mini-cars, with racing tracks on the sixth floor.

Mr. Craft floor list: **1F** new toys, **2F** F1 race cars, **3F** mini-cars, **4F** events, **5F** showcase shop, **6F** racing paradise Ebisu (www.banproject.com)

MANGART   11
19-6-2F, SHARUGAKUCHO, SHIBUYA-KU
03-5428-5952
HOURS: 11:00 — 20:00

Yet another of the many offshoot arms of Beams, Mangart specializes in tees and accessories all based around — you guessed it — manga. From classic characters to current-day, cute, mean, robotic, and scantily clad, Mangart offers up all sorts of variations on the theme for any discriminating fan or hipster.

ZAC-PAC   08
16-2, DAIKANYAMA, SHIBUYA-KU
03-5428-6164
HOURS: 12:00 — 20:00

A fun-filled variety toy store overflowing with cute creations, as well as action figures and the occasional vinyl, Zac-Pac is a catchall for anyone and everyone looking for a little something to give as a gift or searching for the unexpected, from Rody to Rat Fink to everything in between.

DEVILOCK / LET IT RIDE   13/14

Two of the more distinct fashion brands in Tokyo, Devilock and Let It Ride are also very popular with Western travelers. Devilock is based upon a rich punk history mixed with current trends and fashion (the name being a Misfits reference), while Let It Ride takes its inspiration from outlaw bikers from the '60s. With Japanese artist NUTS providing most of the signage in Let It Ride, it is hard to believe that the displays are new and not authentic vintage.

EBISU/DAIKANYAMA

10
STITCH
11-8, SARUGAKUCHO, SHIBUYA-KU

A store based on the art of lifestyle and design goods, Stitch specializes in home furnishings, including art and toys. While the front of the shop may deceive you with furniture, the back shop houses a small art gallery with revolving shows featuring many up-and-coming artists from around the globe. Additionally, it is one of the first shops in Japan to actively promote group custom-toy shows, and regularly has exclusive product made for its shop or specialty shows. With a focus on designers over brands or styles, Stitch crosses over into a more traditionally "Western" style of toy than most Japanese shops.

- HIGHLIGHT SHOPS
- SECONDARY SHOPS
- POINTS OF INTEREST
- LANDMARKS
- KOBAN POLICE

YAMANOTE

KEIO-INAKASHIRA LINE

SHIMOKITAZAWA

Shimokitazawa is off the beaten path, yet somehow is mysteriously filled with Western tourists, who are most likely not here to see the toy shops. Both sides of the station are filled with small new and used shops, most focusing on clothing, and the occasional sneaker shop, with a little bit of everything else thrown in for good measure. It can be difficult to get your bearings at first in Shimokitazawa, a confusing maze of small, windy streets, with two intersecting train lines making it even trickier.

With its eclectic mix of shops, Shimokitazawa is a fun destination for a leisurely afternoon of walking, but visitors in a hurry will not benefit from it, as you will be conveniently located next to absolutely nothing while here.

To reach Shimokitazawa, located just four quick stops from Shibuya on the private Keio-Inakashira line, you will need to exit the JR train station at Shibuya and follow the signs over the footbridge to the Keio lines across from the train station. (See the Shibuya map on page 39 for more details.) More advanced travelers can also take the private Odakyu line six stops from Shinjuku, but navigating that train station is up to you. Departing from Shibuya makes it easy, because the train line terminates there, so there is no possibility of boarding a train going in the wrong direction.

01_ B MANIACS **02_** HARDCORE CHOCOLATE (2F) **03_** GRANIPH **04_** SUNNY CO. **05-A/B_** DORAMA **06_** 2X2=8
07_ ZEMBA SHOHTEN **08_** FUNNY FANNY **09_** HOME-RICE **10_** TOYS PARADISE **11_** SOUNDS GOOD
12_ VILLAGE VANGUARD **13_** NATUKA SHIA **14_** FEWTURE SHOP/PLANET-X **15_** WARUGAKI SALON

Shimokitazawa Map

- 01
- 02
- 03
- 04
- 05A
- 05B
- 06
- 07
- 08
- 09
- 10
- 11
- 12
- 13
- 14

SHIMOKITAZAWA SIGN

SHIMOKITAZAWA STATION

EXIT

LAWSON'S

MR. DONUT

ODAKYU

KEIO-INAKASHIRA

Upon arriving in Shimokitazawa, exit the train station at the south exit, where you'll be right in the thick of things. The exit is fairly congested and the streets are laid out at slightly awkward angles, so walk more or less "straight" and take a right onto one of Shimokitazawa's main streets. One block down, turn left and walk half a block farther, where you will see a small alley to the left with several shops. In the back right corner is B Maniacs (01), which sells mostly old paper goods, and upstairs is Hardcore Chocolate (02), an oddball fashion t-shirt company, mixing random horror movie and punk rock images, that Quentin Tarantino apparently loves.

Back on the street, fashion t-shirt shop Graniph is on the left (03), and just a few stores down is Sunny Co. (04), a shop with all the latest in toy and model-kit releases. Next door to Sunny Co., on the corner and across the street, is Dorama (05A, 05B), which offers a great selection of used books. If you are hungry, take a right and head down two blocks to 2x2=8 (06). Located on the second floor, this is an all-you-can-eat Indian restaurant for 900 yen per person, but watch out—the drinks are 300 yen apiece and can drive your price up quickly.

Strolling back down the main road, pass Mr. Donut, and after two blocks, you will see Zemba Shohten (07) on the left, an old-school candy and toy store where you never know what to expect. Just down a narrow side street to the right is Funny Fanny (08), which focuses mostly on small toys, Smurfs, and *Peanuts* characters. Taking a right at the next fork will get you to Home-Rice (09), on the left-hand side. An amazing vintage-toy shop with phenomenal prices, Home-Rice is another of Tokyo's great secrets.

Back on the main drag once again, one more block down on the left is Toys Paradise (10). Looking more like a generic toy store on the outside, Toys Paradise has vintage figures hidden throughout the shop, and cheap gifts of all sizes.

As you return to the train station, turn right and walk along the tracks to the crossover point. To the right, half a block down, is Village Vanguard (12), a purveyor of cheap novelty gifts and books and a favorite shop for artists looking for odd titles from obscure Japanese illustrators.

After you cross the tracks and under the Shimokitazawa sign (shown at left), Natuka Shia (13) is just one and a half blocks up. Located above Zappas, Natuka Shia is a hit-or-miss vintage shop. As you continue one more block, turn left, then walk several blocks down the road to Fewture Shop/Planet-X (14), located just off the main street. The house shop for the Fewture Company, it is full of new and vintage toys but has very limited hours. Even farther up the road is Warugaki Salon (15), a Doraemon collectors' heaven.

For those not wanting to miss anything in Shimokitazawa, Sounds Good (11) is located on the other side of the station. Featuring advertising characters and Hawaiiana, this fun little shop is right off the main street and is indicative of Shimokitazawa's eclectic nature. If you have time, we recommend wandering up and down all the side streets in this neighborhood; something new and unexpected always seems to pop up.

WARUGAKI SALON 15
3-34-4 KITAZAWA KU SETAGAYA
03-3460-1739, BLOG.LIVEDOOR.JP/DAGASIYA63/
HOURS: 18:00 — 3:00

This is a small shop that specializes in Doraemon toys, candy, and other toys of yesteryear. The man who runs it, known as Doraemon Uncle, has a blog all about his daily life, and an obsession with horse racing. Warugaki Salon roughly translates to "naughty boys' place", so take that as you see fit.

FEWTURE SHOP/PLANET-X 14
3-31-14 KITAZAWA, SETAGAYA-KU
03-3460-9742, ARTSTORM.CO.JP/SHOP.HTM
HOURS: FRIDAY & SATURDAY 13:00 — 20:00

Planet-X is the retail shop attached to toy manufacturer Fewture. There are vintage and new toys, along with Fewture products, and rumor has it that all the vintage comes from a secret warehouse that Fewture owns. Planet-X is open only on Fridays and Saturdays, so plan accordingly.

09

HOME-RICE
5-29-9 DAIZAWA, SETAGAYA-KU
03-3411-5262
HOURS: 12:00 — 19:30

Often referred to as "Oma Rise," Home-Rice is one of Tokyo's best one-stop shops. Carrying a little bit of everything, including tin, die-cast, advertising, twelve-inch figures, jumbos, and vinyl, it is just as enjoyable for looking at toys as it is for buying them. With a helpful and knowledgeable staff and some of the best prices in the city, Home-Rice is one of Tokyo's toy hunters' secret spots.

SHIMOKITAZAWA

ZEMBA SHOHTEN — 07
5-36-7 DAIZAWA, SETAGAYA-KU,
03-3414-2079
HOURS: 13:00 — 20:00, CLOSED THURSDAY

In this classic candy store, there are toys tucked here, there, and everywhere. Everything appears random, and if there is a method to their madness, we haven't figured it out. If you were a kid today, this might be your favorite store, but if you are prone to cavities, stay away.

NATUKA SHIA — 13
2-31-14 KITAZAWA, SETAGAYA-KU
03-3485-1294, WWW.SHIMOKITAZAWA.NET/I/421.HTML
HOURS: 12:30 — 20:00, CLOSED TUESDAY

Situated above the shop Zappas is another one of Tokyo's older shops, Natuka Shia. Smaller and more cramped than most of Shimokitazawa's shops, it still has plenty to see. Natuka Shia is exclusively for collectors; vintage is all that is available. Most of the stock seems to have been there for quite some time, and new stock does not seem to arrive as quickly as it does in other stores. We recommend visiting if you can, as this shop may not last much longer.

SOUNDS GOOD — 11
2-23-6 SETAGAYA, KITAZAWA
03-5433-3758, WWW.HOME.ATT.NE.JP/GREEN/SOUNDSGOOD
HOURS: 13:00 — 20:00

A small shop covered in corrugated metal and display signs, Sounds Good is home to a decent sampling of advertising character toys and Hawaii-oriented merchandise. Although we have never known anyone to actually buy anything in this fun little shop, it sure looks nice.

10
TOYS PARADISE
5-30-3 DAIZAWA, SETAGAYA-KU
03-3419-7256
HOURS: 12:00 — 20:00, CLOSED MONDAY

A mixture of old and new, character and kaiju, Toys Paradise looks like a cheap toy store at first glace but has many hidden gems lying in wait. This is a shop where digging around pays off, as sometimes even the store owner can't remember where everything is. Claiming to be the third-oldest toy store in all of Japan, Toys Paradise has been around forever, but we don't actually know how long forever is. The store owner is one of the nicest you will ever meet, and while the selection may be suspect, your visit is sure to be pleasant.

SUNNY CO.   04
2-12-1 KITAZAWA, SETAGAYA-KU
03-3413-0857, WWW.HOBBYSHOP-SUNNY.COM
HOURS: 10:00 — 21:00, CLOSED THE 2ND AND 3RD TUESDAY

The only two-story toy shop in Shimokitazawa, Sunny Co.'s bottom floor is dominated by model kits, and the second floor houses new Bandai releases and the latest in vinyl and chogokin. While there is nothing here that you won't find at other new toy stores, you may find something here that was sold out in more highly trafficked neighborhoods.

DORAMA   05A / 05B
2-12-16 KITAZAWA, SETAGAYA-KU
03-3487-4233, WWW.DORAMA.CO.JP
HOURS: 13:00 — 20:00

While there are several Dorama shops in the Shimokitazawa area, the bookstore immediately to the left of Sunny Co. seems to be the best (05A). Filled with tons of used books and magazines, as well as the occassional toy, it is worth a stop if you are in the area. Dorama (05B), across the street, usually sells movies, but changes every so often to a different kind of stock.

FUNNY FANNY   08
5-33-3 DAIZAWA, SETAGAYA-KU
03-5481-3857, WWW.FUNNYFANNY.BIZ
HOURS: 13:00 — 20:00

Focusing on cute character goods like Snoopy, the Smurfs, and Disneyana, Funny Fanny has tons of PVC desktop collectibles for collectors from five to fifty. Though it's far from our area of expertise, there is always someone shopping here, so they must be doing something right.

SINGLE-STOP TOY SHOPS

MACHIYA
AOTO
EKODA
TOYS-R-US

TOY FESTIVALS

- HIGHLIGHT SHOPS
- SECONDARY SHOPS
- POINTS OF INTEREST
- LANDMARKS
- KOBAN POLICE

YAMANOTE

SŌBU LOCAL

CHIYODA LINE

MACHIYA

C17

SUBWAY STATIONS:
EACH STOP ON THE TOKYO METRO SUBWAY IS NUMBERED AND EACH LINE IS LETTER CODED FOR YOUR CONVENIENCE. THE CHIYODA LINE IS INDICATED BY A LETTER "C," THE HANZOMAN LINE BY A "Z," AND THE TOZAI LINE BY A "T," AMONG OTHERS. THIS WAY, YOU ALWAYS KNOW EXACTLY WHICH LINE AND STOP YOU ARE AT, NO MATTER WHERE YOU ARE.

Machiya is another small neighborhood that most toy collectors have not visited. As it is well off the beaten path, going to Machiya requires taking the JR Yamanote line to Nishi-Nippori, then transferring to the Tokyo Metro Subway system and the Chiyoda line. One stop up the Chiyoda line (Nishi-Nippori is denoted by stop C16) is Machiya (stop C17).

Take Exit 1, and you should be at a street corner by the SMBC building and the Koban. If you don't see them, walk around the station until you do, or ask where the Koban is. From there, take a right-hand turn and walk one very short block to the first right, then one and a half quick blocks down. On the right-hand side is Jyarinco (01), indicated by two small signs in Japanese that say "antique toy" in English. Located on the second floor, Jyarinco is packed with just about every kind of toy imaginable, including more Jumbo Machinders than anywhere else in the city. The prices here are incredible, and even better for toys in imperfect condition. Additionally, much like Koenji's Ichiban-Boshi, Jyarinco collaborated with RealxHead to create the Devil Dog and Cyclops Dog figures that were released exclusively through this shop.

MACHIYA

JYARINCO   01
1-20-9 MACHIYA, ARAKAWA-KU
03-3893-4045, WWW.JYARINCO.COM
HOURS: 12:30 — 20:30

An amazing store with every conceivable kind of toy in stock, Jyarinco is the last of Tokyo's hidden gems. Because it is tucked away in Machiya, few make the trek to Jyarinco, but those who do are rewarded with great deals. Focusing more on vinyl than on die-casts, and featuring a good Jumbo Machinder selection, Jyarinco has a little something for everyone. Not much else is in the area, so it is usually the first or last stop of the day for toy hunters.

- HIGHLIGHT SHOPS
- SECONDARY SHOPS
- POINTS OF INTEREST
- LANDMARKS
- KOBAN POLICE

YAMANOTE

KEISEI

MUTANTS AMONG US: INVISIBLE TO HUMANS, THE MUTANTS OF REALXHEAD (HEAD, EVIL, BIGARO, AND CHAOS) ARE FIGHTING TO SAVE MANKIND FROM THE EVIL MUTANT AKRO-KAIZER AND HIS FOLLOWERS. THE BATTLE OF THE MUTANTS HAS JUST BEGUN — NOW YOU HAVE TO DECIDE WHICH SIDE YOU ARE ON.

AOTO

Hiding seven stops out on the Keisei line, Aoto is a quiet residential neighborhood and a surprising spot to find one of Tokyo's most up-and-coming brands. Housed in the neighborhood in which they live, RealxHead and its founder, Mori-Kun (Katsura), have opened their own shop to highlight their brand. Flocked to by loyal fans for every release, the RealxHead shop boasts casefuls of figures, from test shots to prototypes, as well as one of every figure released to date. To get there, head to the Aoto exit (there is only one) and turn left at the gates and then left again to cross over to the other side of the tracks. Immediately turn right, and follow the tracks down three streets until you see a slightly diagonal street on the left. Head up two blocks, and the RealxHead shop is on the corner.

AOTO

REALxHEAD   01
6-4-15-101, AOTO, KATSUSHIKA CITY
03-3690-9353, WWW.REALXHEAD.JP
HOURS: WED. — SUN. 18:00 — 21:00

For fans of modern kaiju and fight figures, RealxHead needs no introduction. For the rest of you, RealxHead is a promising boutique toy brand whose main characters are a mutant mix of new and old monster influence. As much a museum as it is a store, the RealxHead shop offers a lot of eye candy, but releases are (by design) in short supply. Hardcore collectors call daily for the latest release updates, while at least one figure is always guaranteed to be available for anyone showing up any other time.

▌	**HIGHLIGHT SHOPS**
▌	**SECONDARY SHOPS**
▌	**POINTS OF INTEREST**
■	**LANDMARKS**
★	**KOBAN POLICE**

YAMANOTE

SŌBU LOCAL

SEIBU-IKEBUKURO

EKODA

Lovely little Ekoda, almost no one knows your name. Hiding on the private Seibu Ikebukuro line, it is such a small stop, many maps don't even list it. Now home to the shop Cosmo Knight Alpha (formerly of Shinjuku), Ekoda is a requisite stop for vinyl collectors.

To get there, take the JR Yamanote line to Ikebukuro and leave the JR system, transferring to the private Seibu Ikebukuro line. Just three stops down the line, the small (and usually unlabeled) Ekoda is quite unassuming. (Make sure you take a local train and not an express, or it will pass Ekoda.) Take the north exit from the station, then take a left, following the tracks.

When you reach the crossover for the tracks, turn right, walking up two and a half blocks until you see a glass sliding door stacked full of vinyl. This is Cosmo Knight Alpha (01), home to more than a few of the rarest vinyls we have seen in years, as well as plenty of much more affordable figures. The shop is packed, and although the staff speak no English, they are very nice and well versed in vinyl minute.

On the way back to the train station is an action figure and t-shirt shop called Bandit (02), just on the other side of the tracks and two blocks over. This is only worth your time if you are a toy-shop-tour completist or are really into action figures. Most people simply get back on the train and return to Ikebukuro.

TODAY AND YESTERDAY: THE CORNERSTONES OF COSMO NIGHT ALPHA'S SUCCESS — A NEW BEMON RELEASE ON THE LEFT, ALONGSIDE A STAGGERINGLY RARE BAGGED IKB MOSUGON ON THE RIGHT. IF YOU UNDERSTAND WHY HE IS HOLDING THESE TWO TOYS, THEN THIS IS THE SHOP FOR YOU.

EKODA

COSMO KNIGHT ALPHA   01
25-17 1F NERIMA SAKAE
03-3557-4616, WWW.SOFVI.COM
HOURS: 12:00 — 20:00

One of the best vintage-vinyl shops in all of Tokyo, CosmoKnight Alpha is a wonderful little store tucked away in Ekoda. Off the beaten path for most collectors, it is a vinyl toy lover's paradise. Lined with cases full of rare hero and kaiju vinyls, as well as a decent selection of die-cast toys, Cosmo Knight Alpha always has a few toys you will probably never see again on display. In addition to their staggering vintage selection, Cosmo Knight Alpha is also the most common release spot for new Japanese company Bemon. Although the shop owner may be stoic and speaks little English, he is quite friendly. Cash is preferred, but credit cards are accepted for larger toy purchases.

Toys-R-Us

For many toy collectors, the thought of being able to walk into a store like Toys-R-Us and see rows of Godzilla, Ultraman, and Gundam hanging next to Star Wars and Hot Wheels is mind-blowing. It almost seems too easy, like some sort of cheat code for collecting Japanese toys. There are several Toys-R-Us stores in the greater Tokyo area, but these three are en route to the other shops in this book.

IKEBUKURO
After a short walk within the Ikebukuro train station, look for the Sunshine City Mall exit and follow it outside. When you finally make this exit, you will need to cross the street and go up the main road, on your right. Look for Tokyu Hands a couple of blocks down. At the entrance to Tokyu Hands is an escalator to the basement, and a underground walkway to Sunshine City Mall. This is another longish walk. When you finally get to Sunshine City Mall, the Toys-R-Us is all the way at the back left of the mall.

ODAIBA
Along the Kuramamome monorail path headed to Tokyo Big Sight, Odaiba is home to the Aqua City Shopping Mall and a scaled-down reproduction of the Statue of Liberty. (Don't ask us why—it's just what happens in Japan sometimes.) Just across the street from the Statue of Liberty is the Kua 'Aina burger joint on the second floor, and an escalator to Toys-R-Us in the basement.

KAMEIDO
On the Sobu line, four stops past Akihabara (and three stops before Koiwa), there is a Toys-R-Us in the open-air shopping mall just south of the train station. The Toys-R-Us is located in the very back of the mall, a bit hidden away when you first enter.

For information about other Toys-R-Us stores, check www.toysrus.co.jp/truj/store/english/stores/kanto/index.html.

OF SPACE AND TIME: FOR SOME REASON, TOYS-R-US IN TOKYO ALWAYS SEEMS TO HAVE THE LATEST STAR WARS ACTION FIGURES AND TOYS WELL BEFORE THE SAME CHAIN IN THE UNITED STATES. EVEN MORE CONFUSING IS THE FACT THAT THEY SEEMINGLY HAVE AN ENDLESS SUPPLY AS WELL. APPARENTLY THE FORCE IS STRONG IN TOKYO, AND TOYS-R-US IS A JEDI MASTER.

VARIOUS TOYS-R-US STORES

IKEBUKURO, TOYS-R-US
3-1 HIGASHIIKEBUKURO, TOSHIMA-KU (LOCATED IN SUNSHINE CITY MALL)
03-3983-5400, WWW.TOYSRUS.CO.JP/TRUJ/STORE/ENGLISH/STORES/KANTO/ST_IBSUNSHINE.HTML
HOURS: 10:00 — 20:00

ODAIBA, TOYS-R-US
1-7-1 ODAIBA, MINATO-KU (LOCATED IN ODAIBA DECKS AREA)
03-5564-5011, WWW.TOYSRUS.CO.JP/TRUJ/STORE/ENGLISH/STORES/KANTO/ST_ODAIBA.HTML
HOURS: 10:00 — 20:00

KAMEIDO, TOYS-R-US
6-31-1 KAMEIDO, KOTO-KU (LOCATED IN SUN STREET SHOPPING CENTER)
04-7347-2335, WWW.TOYSRUS.CO.JP/TRUJ/STORE/ENGLISH/STORES/KANTO/ST_KAMEIDO.HTML
HOURS: 10:00 — 20:00

Toy Festivals

Many travelers to Tokyo like to synchronize their trip with an event, such as a toy show. In Tokyo, four kinds of toy shows happen at different times of the year. All vary slightly in their coverage, and they all happen at one of two locations: Tokyo Big Sight or the Science Museum Hall. The events always occur on Sundays, and you can usually be finished with a show by 1:00 or 2:00 PM, which gives you ample time to get to other areas of the city.

THE FOUR KINDS OF SHOWS ARE:

WONDER FESTIVAL: The biggest show of the year, Wonder Festival is an all-encompassing event that highlights new toys and model kits above all others. There is very little vintage at this show. What is unique about Wonder Festival is that many companies grant one-day licenses to myriad small companies to make unique one-off toys and models that will never be seen again. The show is held at Tokyo Big Sight, and collectors line up more than twenty-four hours in advance to get their hands on the show's exclusives. Show dates are listed at www.kaiyodo.co.jp/wf.

WORLD CHARACTER CONVENTION: Commonly referred to as WCC, this show features a decent mix of both vintage and newer toys, but only a smattering of exclusives. Unofficially known as the blowout and inexpensive show, this is an event that many dealers use to get rid of excess stock at rock-bottom prices, but it is usually the less popular toys left over from the last few years of releases. Held at Tokyo Big Sight. Show dates are listed at www.wcc-jp.com.

TOKYO TOY FESTIVAL: Traditionally a vintage-only show, Tokyo Toy Festival originally occurred in conjunction with Wonder Festival, but recently has been held on the following weekend. The smallest of all the shows, it is held at Tokyo Big Sight. Show dates are listed at www.toyfes.jp.

SUPER FESTIVAL: A vintage toy show, and the only show held at the Science Museum. Run by Artstorm/Fewture, it happens on a regular basis, always has a fair amount of exclusives, and usually a special guest of some noteriety. Toy dealers new and old come out, as well as most boutique manufacturers. Lines begin forming around four in the morning, with two sets of lines—one for entrance into the show, and another for show-exclusive toys, which are sold in a slightly different area. Selection can vary dramatically from show to show, but there is usually something good for everyone. Show dates are listed at www.artstorm.co.jp/sufes.html.

RISE AND SHINE:
IF YOU PLAN ON BUYING ANY OF THE MORE SOUGHT-AFTER TOY EXCLUSIVES AT ANY TOY SHOW, WE RECOMMEND SHOWING UP EARLY. LINES CAN START FORMING AS EARLY AS SIX TO TWENTY-FOUR HOURS IN ADVANCE — BUT YOU'LL PROBABLY BE UP BY 6:00 ANYWAY.

TOY FESTIVALS

DIRECTIONS TO TOKYO BIG SIGHT:
Take the JR Yamanote line to Shimbashi Station. Look for the Yurikamome Monorail exit. As you exit the JR station, turn right out of the turnstiles. The Yurikamome entrance will be directly in front of you; purchase a ticket to Kokusai-Tenjijo. Shimbashi is the end of the line, so you don't have to worry about getting on a train going the wrong direction. Along the route, you will pass Odaiba Station, which is home to Toys-R-Us. (Most showgoers stop here on their way back from the show, to grab a bite from Kua 'Aina burger and shop at Toys-R-Us.) Upon arriving at Kokusai-Tenjijo, walk across the pathway to the giant inverted triangle known as Tokyo Big Sight. There will be plenty of signs, people, and lines directing you to exactly where you should go. For more information, go to www.bigsight.jp/english/general/access/index.html.

DIRECTIONS TO THE SCIENCE MUSEUM:
From Shibuya, take the Tokyo Metro Subway Hanzoman line (purple) six stops to Kudanshita. Shibuya is the last stop on the Hanzoman line, so you don't have to worry about going the wrong direction. (Kudanshita is also indicated by stop Z6.) At Kudanshita, transfer to the Tokyo Metro Subway Tozai line. You will be at stop T7, and you will need to go one stop to Takabashi, stop T8. At Takabashi, take exit 1B and go west, past the Museum of Modern Art and the National Archives. Turn right on the main road, and follow the signs to the Science Museum, which is located right next to the legendary music hall Budokan. For more information, go to www.jsf.or.jp/eng/map.

CONCLUSION

That just about wraps it up for us. If you want to know more, we encourage you to seek it out, as we have run dry. (Okay, we may have kept one or two secrets to ourselves, but we aren't telling.) Along the way, if you notice shops that have closed or moved, or new shops we should know about, don't hesitate to let us know (contact information is on the copyright page). Tell the shop owners how you got there. Show them this book; ask them to sign their pictures. Strike up a conversation, buy some toys, and have a fun trip. You don't get to Tokyo very often, so make it a memorable experience.

BRIAN FLYNN
Brian Flynn was born in the midst of a hurricane in 1875. After spending his formative years underachieving at various tasks, he decided the world was not ready for his forward-thinking vision of the future and was cryogenically frozen until 1994. After reawakening, Brian hit the streets, and decided that ruling the universe through the hidden mysticism of arcane Star Wars references, binary pulsar radio-emission patterns, vintage Japanese vinyls, and Coca-Cola was the only way to go. Brian is the publisher and owner of *Super7* magazine, a partner and founder of Hybrid Design, an award-winning designer, and a highly obsessed toy collector.

JEFF DEY
Born outside of Detroit but growing up a stone's throw from NASA in Clear Lake, Texas, Jeff Dey spent his early years obsessing over rockets, spaceships, Batman, a certain dark-haired drama class girl, and losing to Lance Armstrong in bicycle races. After graduating with a design degree and becoming a design director for Nike, Jeff turned to the allure of elaborate photo shoots, realized a childhood dream of going to NASA's neutral buoyancy lab, and exceeded his mother's expectations. Jeff is currently in an exotic locale, shooting beautiful photographs and making bad jokes.

JOSHUA BERNARD
Joshua Bernard was born in Lowell, Massachusetts, in May of 1973. Like many children born at that time, he was raised by *Speed Racer*, *Force Five*, and George Lucas. In 2001, his obsession for Japanese toys and culture caused him to create CollectionDX.com, a popular website for toy collecting. Since then, he has written for *Super7* magazine and made the pilgrimage to Tokyo on several occasions. Joshua currently lives in Massachusetts with his wife, four children, two cats, two guinea pigs, and several dozen fish.

PK730

こんなにオススメ!
からだが疲れて、グッタリする
熱があって、寒気がする
食欲がない…
そんな時の栄養補給に
リコリスZ ¥840
3本入 ¥840

sato
HEALTHCARE INNOVATION

PLACES YOU ARE STAYING IN JAPAN (HOTEL, RESIDENCE ETC.)

NAME:

PHONE 1:   PHONE 2:

EMAIL 1:   EMAIL 2:

ADDRESS:

NOTES:

NAME:

PHONE 1:   PHONE 2:

EMAIL 1:   EMAIL 2:

ADDRESS:

NOTES:

NAME:

PHONE 1:   PHONE 2:

EMAIL 1:   EMAIL 2:

ADDRESS:

NOTES:

DON'T FORGET TO DO:

- [ ]
- [ ]
- [ ]
- [ ]
- [ ]
- [ ]
- [ ]
- [ ]
- [ ]
- [ ]
- [ ]
- [ ]
- [ ]
- [ ]
- [ ]
- [ ]
- [ ]
- [ ]
- [ ]
- [ ]
- [ ]
- [ ]
- [ ]
- [ ]

DON'T FORGET TO DO:

DAILY PLAN	MM / DD / YY	
PAGE #	🕐	ACTIVITIES

DAILY PLAN MM / DD / YY

PAGE #	🕐	ACTIVITIES

DAILY PLAN MM / DD / YY

PAGE #	🕐	ACTIVITIES

DAILY PLAN MM / DD / YY

PAGE #	🕐	ACTIVITIES

TRACK YOUR EXPENSES

DATE MM / DD / YY	YEN ¥	SPENT ON:
/ /	¥	
/ /	¥	
/ /	¥	
/ /	¥	
/ /	¥	
/ /	¥	
/ /	¥	
/ /	¥	
/ /	¥	
/ / .	¥	
/ /	¥	
/ /	¥	
/ /	¥	
/ /	¥	
/ /	¥	
/ /	¥	
/ /	¥	
/ /	¥	
/ /	¥	
	DAMAGE ¥	

TRACK YOUR EXPENSES

DATE MM / DD / YY	YEN ¥	SPENT ON:
/ /	¥	
/ /	¥	
/ /	¥	
/ /	¥	
/ /	¥	
/ /	¥	
/ /	¥	
/ /	¥	
/ /	¥	
/ /	¥	
/ /	¥	
/ /	¥	
/ /	¥	
/ /	¥	
/ /	¥	
/ /	¥	
/ /	¥	
/ /	¥	
/ /	¥	
/ /	¥	
/ /	¥	
DAMAGE	¥	

TRACK YOUR EXPENSES

DATE MM / DD / YY	YEN ¥	SPENT ON:
/ /	¥	
/ /	¥	
/ /	¥	
/ /	¥	
/ /	¥	
/ /	¥	
/ /	¥	
/ /	¥	
/ /	¥	
/ /	¥	
/ /	¥	
/ /	¥	
/ /	¥	
/ /	¥	
/ /	¥	
/ /	¥	
/ /	¥	
/ /	¥	
/ /	¥	
	DAMAGE ¥	

TRIP JOURNAL   /   /

TRIP JOURNAL   /   /

TRIP JOURNAL   /   /

TRIP JOURNAL   /   /